Croquet

Croquet

J.W. SOLOMON

A & C Black · London

Published in paperback 1989 by
A & C Black (Publishers) Ltd
35 Bedford Row, London WC1R 4JH

First published 1966 by B.T. Batsford Ltd, London
Republished 1983 by EP Publishing Ltd, Wakefield

ISBN 0 7136 5636 0

A CIP catalogue record for this book is available
from the British Library.

Printed and bound in Great Britain by
Hollen Street Press Ltd of Slough

Contents

Acknowledgment

The author and publisher would like to thank Peter Alvey for his kind permission to reproduce the cover photograph and all black-and-white photographs throughout the book.

The author's achievements

Open Champion 1953, 1956, 1959, 1961, 1963, 1964, 1965, 1966, 1967, 1968
Men's Champion 1951, 1953, 1958, 1959, 1960, 1962, 1964, 1965, 1971, 1972
Open Doubles Champion (with E.P.C. Cotter) 1954, 1955, 1958, 1959, 1961-2-3-4-5, 1969
President's Cup 1955, 1957, 1958, 1959, 1962, 1963, 1964, 1968, 1971
Open Championship (New Zealand) 1951, 1963
Open Doubles Championship (New Zealand) 1951 (with H.O. Hicks), 1963 (with E.P.C. Cotter)
Open Doubles Championship (Victoria, Australia) 1951 (with H.O. Hicks)
Mixed Doubles Championship 1954 (with Mrs F. Oddie)
Championship of Champions 1967, 1968, 1969, 1970

Line illustrations

Photographs

Introduction

'I am told you play croquet.' I admit cautiously that croquet is indeed my principal sport whilst I try to assess the opinion which my acquaintance has already secretly formed of me in the light of this information. Is there an amused glint in his eye, a look of bemused incredulity, or are the lips drawn back in an ill-concealed sneer? It might even be that there is a tone of genuine interest, denoting that here is someone who has some real knowledge of what croquet is, or perhaps, more accurately, what croquet is not, for there is probably more ill-conceived opinion about croquet than about any other sport.

It is a widely held opinion that croquet is an amusing little pastime, quite pleasant for half an hour or so, particularly when taken with tea on the lawn or even more particularly when the tea trolley becomes an extra hazard to go round—or even under. Dreadfully vicious, of course, and calculated to bring out the most spiteful traits of one's fellow players.

This view, is, no doubt, a hangover from the days at the turn of the century when a gentle game of croquet was regarded as a much more suitable pastime for the young ladies of the period than tennis, which at that time was little more than patball. Yet when the development of the overarm service transformed tennis into the fast and exciting sport it has become today, croquet also was developing in science and skill. The tragedy was that this transformation was confined to the croquet played in the tournaments and championships organised by the Croquet Association and did not extend to the games played for amusement at home. But it is not my intention to dwell upon the history of croquet, for others are more qualified than I to do so, and a number of books have already been written which record in some detail the history of the game.

Perhaps the reason why croquet is so very much a minor sport is because it is so very difficult, not only in technique but equally so in theory. It is no exaggeration to say that anyone can play tennis, or bowls, or billiards—up to a point—after 10 minutes' instruction, and know enough to play something like the game and get considerable enjoyment from it. Years of practice are necessary, of course, to become expert at these games, but they have a certain advantage in that they can be played almost immediately by a complete novice.

Croquet, perhaps unfortunately, cannot be attempted so easily, for even if we assume that a beginner can in an hour or so grasp enough of the game to understand what he should attempt to do—and it is doubtful whether many beginners do understand even the basic principles of the game in so short a time—it is quite certain that his skill will not match his knowledge for some considerable time. The result is that he is quite unable to perform the manœuvres that he knows he ought to perform. Thus he suddenly discovers that croquet is a very difficult game, and, like all things that present a worthwhile challenge, provides the greatest satisfaction when one's efforts are rewarded.

What, then, is croquet? The simplest description is probably the most misleading. The players attempt to get their balls (for in singles each have two) through all the hoops in the correct order and finally to hit the peg. But to say this gives no indication of what is involved, for it is not merely doing it but *how* it is done, that is remarkable. It is not the fact that a billiard player goes on potting reds or making cannons, but the way in which he manœuvres both his ball and the others, often to a fraction of an inch, that enables him to keep going and makes him a great player. So, in croquet, it is the skill in the execution of the many strokes —roquet, croquet, roll, pass-roll, stop-shot, split-shot, take-off—that enables the player to make not only several, but frequently all his hoops for one of his balls in one turn, while his opponent looks helplessly on from the side-lines, unable to stop him, for perhaps a quarter of an hour, so long as he makes no mistake.

Perhaps already you are finding that croquet is rather different from what you had imagined it to be. You may have pictured it as a game in which the players all stand on the court, playing in sequence and trying to get through the hoops in one stroke, or knocking the others out of position, preferably into the shrubbery. This is *not* croquet, but golf croquet, and has no more resemblance to the real game than draughts has to chess.

Before going into further detail you will no doubt wish to know what it will cost you to play croquet. It is, in fact, very little, for it is probably one of the cheapest sports. The only equipment you will need will be a mallet, a pair of flat-soled shoes and a small subscription to a local club. If you have a good lawn at home you may feel that you will be able to manage quite happily on your own. But it is still well worth while joining a club, for it is only by playing as often as possible against different players, and if possible better ones than yourself, that you will really learn the game.

Learning the language

Before we can find out how the game is played, we must get quite clear in our minds the basic facts of the court and its accessories, the names of the strokes and the terms employed in croquet.

The Court

A full-sized croquet court measures 35 by 28 yards, much bigger than most people imagine. It is considerably larger than a tennis court and should be as level and true as a bowling green, although unfortunately it is all too rarely that one is lucky enough to find one on which so much attention is lavished. A plan of the court is given on page 12, and you will see that there are six hoops and one central peg. (The setting with two pegs went out years ago!) The balls have to be played through each hoop twice, once in each direction. Each hoop therefore has two numbers. On the outward course they are numbered 1–6 and on the homeward run 1-back, 2-back, 3-back, 4-back, penultimate and rover. There are four boundaries called North, South, East and West, and if we stand in the middle of the South boundary the hoop nearest us to the left with a blue crown is the 1st hoop. We have to make it in the direction in which we are facing and then go straight ahead to the 2nd hoop. Then back down the other two outer hoops, the 3rd and 4th, towards the South boundary again, and from there up the middle, the 5th and 6th hoops, ignoring the peg—and we have completed the first half of the course. We now have to make them all in the opposite direction, the 2nd (which becomes 1-back), 2-back (the 1st), 3-back (4th), 4-back (3rd), and then down the middle again, penultimate (6th) and rover (5th). The rover is painted red to distinguish it as the last hoop, and so if we go on to a strange court we can tell by the colours of the 1st and last hoops which way round we are. Finally, of course, we hit the peg, but we are getting a little ahead of ourselves.

In each corner there is a flag, and one yard along each boundary from the flag is a small peg. These pegs mark the yard-line, an imaginary line running round the court one yard inside the boundary line. Any ball which goes off the court is placed on the yard-line opposite the point at which it crossed the boundary.

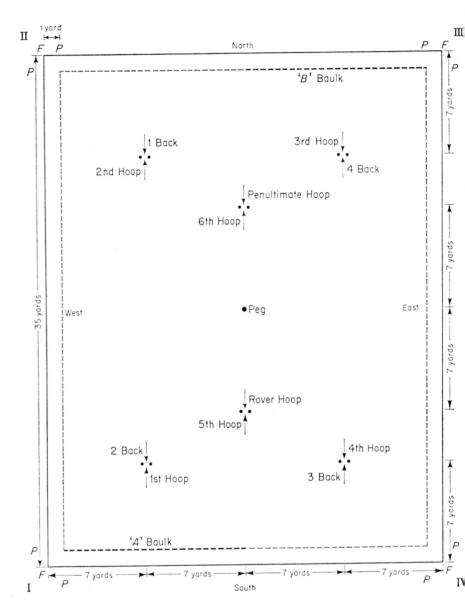

I *The standard court and setting*
(P—corner pegs; F—corner flags)

There is one more point to take note of, and that is the baulk-lines; it is from these that the game begins. The A baulk is that part of the yard-line which runs from the middle of the South boundary to the 1st corner spot and the B baulk is complementary to it, being that part of the yard-line from the middle of the North boundary to the 3rd corner spot.

Hoops

The hoops are of round iron $\frac{5}{8}$ inch thick, have a square crown and stand one foot high out of the ground. The width between the inside edges of the uprights is $3\frac{3}{4}$ inches, and although it can be greater than this it is really foolish to play with wider hoops, as the game loses a good deal of its skill. If you are going to buy your own croquet set beware of the description given to some of them. The only hoops worth playing with are usually described as 'championship' hoops, which are made of cast iron, and have thick, angled footings which keep them firm in the ground. Sets described as 'tournament' hoops are quite useless for any serious form of croquet, being made only of bent wire; they are not only difficult to keep at the right width, but are impossible to keep firm in the ground and are thus very much more difficult to go through.

The Peg

The peg is of round wood, $1\frac{1}{2}$ inches in diameter, and stands 18 inches above the ground. It will probably have a detachable portion on the top to hold the clips.

Balls

There are four balls, coloured blue, red, black and yellow. They are made of a composition, weigh one pound each and are $3\frac{5}{8}$ inches in diameter. If you are arithmetical you will see that the hoops are only $\frac{1}{8}$ inch wider than the balls, and yet it is surprising from what acute angles it is possible to go through the hoops. There is in fact one tournament in which the hoops are only $\frac{1}{16}$ inch wider than the balls, and although this tends to weed out the less accurate players it is surprising how little difference it makes.

Clips

There are also four coloured clips corresponding to each of the balls, and these are used to show which hoop each ball next has to make. For the first six hoops it is placed on the crown of the hoop, for the last six on one of the uprights.

Mallets

Mallets come in all shapes and sizes. The shape does not matter very much, but the size, and the weight, does. In fact, the mallet is the most important piece of equipment over which the player has any real choice, and it is vital that he should get one which suits him. Probably the best course is to experiment for at least a season with all the mallets you can beg, borrow or steal (most clubs have a number of old mallets for beginners). As you gain in proficiency your taste in mallets will probably change several times, and it is as well to be sure which kind suits you best before buying a new one. If you are very lucky you may be able to find a second-hand mallet in good condition, for although they do not exactly improve with age like violins, if carefully treated they will certainly last a lifetime.

There is not much to choose between round-headed and square-headed mallets. It is entirely a matter of personal preference. The wood used for the head will be governed by the weight of the mallet, lighter ones being of boxwood and heavier ones of lignum vitae. Because of the expense of lignum, and the difficulty in obtaining seasoned wood, in recent years fibreglass in various forms has been used increasingly, either for the complete head or as end-pieces glued to each face. These are virtually indestructible and will therefore not get chipped or cracked. It is well worth having wooden heads bound in brass, which will limit the damage caused by 'edge-shots' that everyone makes from time to time. The thickness of the head is to some extent also governed by the weight. The most important part of any mallet is the shaft, since it is this which supplies the contact between the hands and the balls. Ash is generally used for shafts, but I find ash shafts dead, and malacca the reverse, this being far too springy and whippy. I prefer hickory for the shaft with a rather narrow lignum head, about $2\frac{1}{4}$ inches square, which allows one to play at a more acute angle through a hoop. The ideal weight is about 3 pounds, but not more than $1\frac{1}{2}$ ounces either side of this figure.

Metal shafts are also now increasingly available, usually of the golf-club variety. The shaft runs from the head for about 15 inches and is then let into a conventional wooden shaft at the top. Alternatively, it can be a full tubular shaft, some one inch in diameter for the complete length, which is then covered in a rubber grip. The disadvantage as far as I am concerned with this shaft and grip is that it is circular, whereas wooden shafts are normally octagonal and one gets used to the ridges formed by each angle and which feel 'comfortable' in the palm. These shafts can be plain wood, but are usually covered in leather, rubber or flannel grips.

The length of the shaft will depend on your style, and here again you may find your style changing every few weeks during your first season. Style will be the subject of a later chapter, and it will be enough for now to say that with the Irish grip a shaft of about two feet eight inches will be long enough, for other styles about three feet; if you are very tall, another inch or so would not be wrong. The main thing is not to have any extra shaft which is never handled, and to choose your length accordingly. The one thing you cannot do is to cut down the shaft of a mallet, as by doing this the whole balance of the mallet will be ruined. A simple way of testing this is to balance it on one finger to find the balancing point, which should be about one-fifth of the distance from the bottom of the head to the top of the shaft.

Many players find a mallet which suits them, then decide that it is either too heavy or too light and either drill holes in the bottom of the head or sink in lead weights to make the necessary adjustment. This will certainly affect the balance of the mallet and, although it may be possible to make some compensating adjustment to the shaft, the only sensible thing is to look around until you find what you want or order one with the exact specifications.

Definitions

The Object of the Game

This is to score all the 12 hoops and the peg point in the correct order with each ball. The side first doing so is the winner. There are therefore 26 points and the score is described as the difference between the full score achieved by the winner and that achieved by the loser. Thus if the loser has not scored a single hoop (which is by no means unusual, particularly in first-class play), the winner has won +26. If the loser has scored, say, 17 points, he has lost −9 (and the winner has won +9). It should be said here that in Australia and New Zealand the scores of games are described rather more longwindedly, but perhaps more logically, as the two scores achieved by each side; thus, 26–0, 26–17, etc.

The Players

If we consider singles only for the moment, the player whose turn it is, is called the striker, and his opponent is the outplayer.

Four balls are always used, in singles each player having two balls. Blue and Black are always partners against Red and Yellow.

The striker strikes, with his mallet, only one of his balls during any turn.

The Turn

The sides play alternate turns. A turn consists initially of one stroke, but this can be extended if that stroke is a roquet or scores a hoop.

A roquet, which is defined immediately following, entitles the striker to two further strokes—a croquet-stroke played with the striker's ball touching the roqueted ball and then one further ordinary stroke (called the continuation stroke). On this continuation stroke the striker may roquet one of the other balls and then take croquet in the same way, *but he may only roquet each ball once.*

Running a hoop entitles the player to another ordinary stroke and also the right to roquet the other three balls again. Thus, every time a hoop is run the sequence of roquet and croquet can begin again and by a combination of these strokes and running hoops (called making a break), the turn can be extended even until the peg is reached.

Roquet

The roquet is the first of the two basic shots in the game. A player makes a roquet when he causes his ball to hit one of the other three balls. At the beginning of a turn the striker must roquet a ball in order to continue. If he fails to do so his turn ends. A roquet is a hit in which one does not intend to send the roqueted ball to any particular spot, for most often it is a long shot in which one is only too happy to make contact, let alone hit it to any exact position.

Rush

A roquet over which one has control is known as a rush or, conversely, a rush is a roquet in which one intends to send the roqueted ball to a particular spot. It might be to a spot only a yard away or it might be to the other end of the court. The line made by your ball and the ball you are going to roquet is known as the rush-line and if you rush the ball along this line it is known, somewhat obviously, as a *straight rush*. If you wish to rush it to one side or other of this line, it is known as a *cut rush*. To be sure of control for the rush, that is to say, to be sure of rushing the ball to the spot you have chosen, the two balls should not be more than one yard apart, and anything over this distance is usually referred to as a long rush; if not exactly fraught with danger it is more often than not a matter of luck whether the shot will come off as intended.

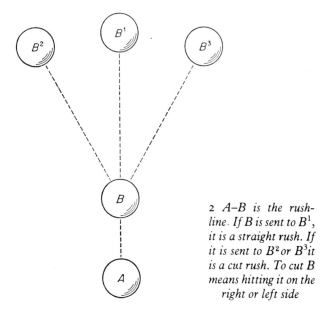

2 *A–B is the rush-line. If B is sent to B^1, it is a straight rush. If it is sent to B^2 or B^3 it is a cut rush. To cut B means hitting it on the right or left side*

Croquet-strokes

Once you have made a roquet you must take croquet. The striker's ball is, for all practical purposes, 'dead' ('in hand' is the technical term), and is picked up—or more probably moved with the feet or the mallet, for croquet can be an exhausting game and it is wise to conserve one's energy—and placed in contact with the roqueted ball, wherever that has come to rest. The croquet-stroke is played by striking your ball with the mallet in such a way that both balls move. That is to say, you cannot hit in a direction away from the croqueted ball (as the roqueted ball is about to become) *nor may you put your foot on your ball* as is often supposed. You can send the croqueted ball to any part of the court by lining the two balls up in the desired direction. You may now strike your ball in any direction up to a right angle on either side of this line, and the croqueted ball will travel in the direction in which it has been aimed. There are two qualifications to be mentioned here, the first being that to aim at right angles to the line along which the croqueted ball is to be sent will almost certainly not shake the croqueted ball and although it need not move *it must at least shake*. It is, however, convenient to refer to the maximum angle at which one can play this stroke as a right angle, although it is in practice two or three degrees less than this. The second is that if you aim to any extent away from the straight line made by the two balls the croqueted ball will not in fact travel quite along this line, but will tend to come round to the side on which you have made the stroke. But this 'pull' is very slight and at this stage you can disregard it.

There are more variations to the croquet-stroke than to any other, and these depend on whether they are degrees of distance or of direction or a combination of both. If we play the stroke in the same direction as we have aimed the two balls, both balls will travel in that direction, but what the stroke is called will depend on how we play it.

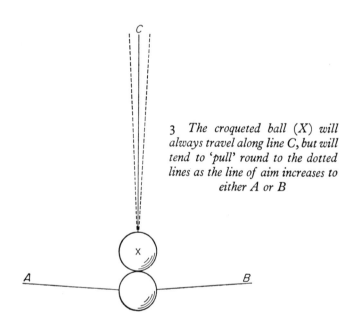

3   *The croqueted ball (X) will always travel along line C, but will tend to 'pull' round to the dotted lines as the line of aim increases to either A or B*

The Roll

If we play the stroke without any follow-through but just let the mallet swing loosely in the hand, the front ball will travel three or four times further than the back ball. If we follow through when playing the stroke, the back ball will travel further in relation to the front ball, when it is a *full roll*. When you are more expert you may even be able to make the back ball go further than the front ball and this is known as a *pass-roll*.

Stop-shot

This is, clearly, the opposite of a pass-roll, in which, by minimising the follow-through of the mallet, the back ball travels a very short distance compared with the front ball. Players with very light mallets have a distinct advantage here and can send the front ball possibly ten times further than the back ball.

Split-shots

So far we have played the croquet-stroke straight but, as was said earlier, we can play it at an angle, and if we do so the back ball will travel away from the croqueted ball also at an angle. What this angle is, is governed by the fairly straightforward rule that the balls will diverge at *twice* the angle at which we are aiming. That is, if we aim at an angle of 15 degrees from the straight, the back ball will go off at 30 degrees from the straight. But we have already said that 90 degrees is the greatest angle of split which it is possible to play, and this is achieved by aiming at an angle of 45 degrees from the straight. If we increase the angle beyond 45 degrees the angle of divergence will not become any greater but instead the distance travelled by the front ball will become less and less.

The Take-off

The take-off is in fact a split-shot played at so wide an angle that the croqueted ball will not travel more than a few feet. It may indeed not move at all, but it must at least shake.

It will be seen that the variation and combination of degrees of split and amount of follow-through *combined in the same stroke* are legion, and the croquet-stroke in all its forms is undoubtedly one of the hardest strokes to master. It is sometimes said that the rush is the most important stroke in the game. It is possible by accurate rushing to play a break without ever playing a split-shot, but really the answer is that both are vital and the player who cannot do one or the other will never be first-class.

Hoop-stroke

Probably the most vital stroke of all is the hoop-stroke, because if we stick in hoops rather than run through them we are not likely to be very successful croquet players. One would not normally think there was much to say about hoop-strokes were it not for the fact that one or two of our better players persist in adopting an exaggerated follow-through designed to impart top-spin, presumably with the idea that if they are not 100 per cent accurate in their aim the spin will carry the ball through. I feel sure that this conscious effort to put on top-spin, which they do not do in any other stroke, causes them to be less accurate in their aim. Certainly those that adopt this practice are notorious for their bad hoop-running, and one would have thought that by now they would have learnt their lesson. There is nothing difficult about hoop-running, one has simply to hit straight!

There is, however, one thing about running hoops which may seem strange. This is that the ball does not have to go all the way through the hoop in order to run it. A ball begins to run a hoop as soon as it can be touched by a straight edge placed against the *non-playing* side of the hoop. Normally, of course, we do not worry about doing this, because we start to run the hoop from the playing side, but if we take position from behind the hoop by running through it, it might have to be tested to be sure that it was on the playing side so that we would now be able to run the hoop. This is done by raising a straight edge (such as a mallet head) up the non-playing side of the hoop. If the ball touches this straight edge it cannot run the hoop—unless of course it originally entered the hoop from the playing side.

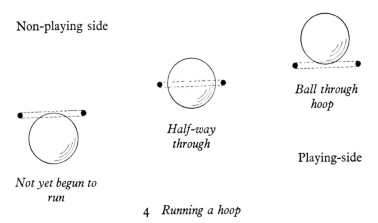

Non-playing side

Half-way through

Ball through hoop

Not yet begun to run

Playing-side

4   *Running a hoop*

In the same way a ball completes the running of a hoop as soon as it cannot be touched by a straight edge raised against the playing side of the hoop.

So much for the strokes themselves. But before we can learn how to string them together there are still one or two facts to get firmly in mind.

Ball off the Court

A ball is off the court as soon as it can be touched by a straight edge raised from the inside of the white line marking the boundary. Thus, for all practical purposes, if a ball overhangs the white line it is off the court and must be placed on the yard-line opposite the point at which it went off. Since the yard-line is not marked on the court it is usual to measure the exact yard with the mallet. It is important to notice that when a ball

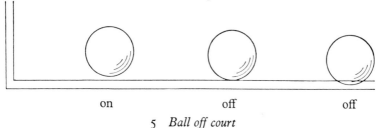

on   off   off

5   *Ball off court*

is going off at a very acute angle to the boundary line it is vital to mark the exact spot, for accuracy in all things is essential in croquet. An error of less than an inch in the placing of a ball can in certain circumstances make a tremendous difference.

The penalties for going off depend upon what kind of shot was played. If on a roquet-stroke either ball goes off, there is no penalty. The roqueted ball is replaced on the yard-line and the striker takes croquet from it. If on a croquet-stroke the croqueted ball goes off, the turn ends. And if on a croquet-stroke the striker's ball goes off, the turn ends *unless* it first makes a roquet or scores its hoop.

Yard-line Area

If any ball ends up between the boundary and the yard-line it must be placed on the yard-line before the next stroke is played. There are two exceptions to this rule (inevitably!). The first and most important is when the striker's ball ends up in the yard-line area after a croquet-stroke. By this means it is possible to get behind a ball on the yard-line and rush it into the court. The second also applies to the striker's ball when it has run a hoop. In both these cases the ball is played from where it lies.

Peel

To peel is to cause a ball (other than the striker's ball) to run its hoop in order.

Triple

Triple is a word which occurs frequently in first-class croquet. The full term is triple peel and it is in fact the description of a turn in which another ball (usually the partner's, but not infrequently an opponent's) is peeled through its last three hoops and pegged out during the course of a normal break with the striker's ball. To say that it is a normal break is perhaps misleading, since some variation is necessary to the standard break to achieve this. The up-and-coming player knows he is approaching the top rank of croquet players when he achieves his first triple peel. There are of course double and single peels, and even more complicated ones: quadruples, quintuples and sextuples which are looked at more fully later on.

How, then, is croquet played? Our first attempt must be to make a roquet, to hit another ball. Having made a roquet we must take croquet from that ball and then have one further shot. If on this we can roquet another ball we repeat the process until we have roqueted each ball once, when we must either run our hoop or our turn ends. If we can run our hoop we can roquet the other three balls again and reach the next hoop. If we fail on any of these strokes, either by missing a roquet, or by sending either ball off on a croquet-stroke, or by sticking in a hoop, our turn ends.

There are two common fallacies to correct at this point. You *may* roquet a ball before you have made the first hoop—indeed, it is practically essential to do so in order to make it at all—and the balls are not played in sequence. The sides play alternately, of course, but you may play either of your balls when you go on to play. Thus you may play with the same ball for several turns running.

Now we have the basic principles at our fingertips let us see how we set about making a break so that we can make all the hoops in one turn.

Breaks

Two-ball Break

The simplest form of break is the two-ball break. It is, however, by far the hardest, since it allows almost no margin of error unless of course one has more luck than anyone deserves. Let us take two balls on to the court.

You are going to play Blue, and we will set the balls up in an easy position so that Black is two yards in front of the 1st hoop and Blue is a foot behind Black. You have a rush on Black to the hoop. You rush Black gently so that it stops about two feet in front of the hoop and six inches or so to one side, let us say the left. Now you must take croquet and approach the hoop, for you cannot hit Black again unless you make the hoop. Put Blue in contact with Black so that they point just to the left-hand side of the hoop. You will find it easier at first to do this with your hand but after a while you will save yourself stooping by doing it nonchalantly with your foot. (This is perhaps why people still imagine that you can put your foot on your ball and send your opponent into the shrubbery. You can't, of course!)

Now you must play the croquet-stroke with a little stop-shot which sends Blue to a spot about six inches in front of the hoop, while the roqueted ball Black, which has now become the croqueted ball, goes five or six feet behind the hoop. You now have one more shot, so you run the hoop just hard enough to stop about a foot behind the Black. You can now roquet the Black again and you have a rush to the 2nd hoop.

But this rush is rather more difficult than the rush to the 1st hoop—this time you have to rush it nearly 20 yards. Still, with a little practice you can do it and with luck the Black will end up a yard or two in front of the 2nd hoop. It does not matter where the Blue goes, because when you have made a roquet it becomes in hand, so pick it up and put it in contact with Black, this time aiming them just to the right of the 2nd hoop. Another little approach shot, not quite such a stop-shot as at the 1st hoop, will send Blue in front of the hoop and Black about two feet past.

Now you have one more shot in which to run the hoop, and you will see why you put Black to the right of the hoop when you approached it.

If you ran the hoop perfectly you now have a perfect rush to the 3rd hoop. Rush Black to the 3rd, approach it as you did the 1st and, after making the hoop, rush Black to the 4th—and so on all the way round the 12 hoops.

Of course, you will by now have realised that every shot has had to be dead accurate or you would have broken down. If, for instance, you had run through the 1st hoop only one foot instead of three or four feet, you would not have been able to swing your mallet to rush Black to the 2nd. On the other hand, if you had run through the hoop too far and gone past Black, you would not have had a rush at all and your only hope would have been to approach the 2nd hoop from the 1st. A roll of about 20 yards with control after the hoop, if you are able to make it at all, is probably worth odds of at least 33–1. This is why the two-ball break is so difficult.

Three-ball Break

Now let us try again, but this time with three balls. Set up Blue and Black as before and put Yellow four feet in front of the 2nd hoop. Roquet Black as before, and approach and run the hoop. You now have a choice. You can either roquet Black gently and then do a big split-shot, sending Black to the 3rd and Blue to Yellow—not a particularly easy shot—or, preferably, rush Black about half-way to the 2nd hoop and do the split from there, which is quite a lot easier. Better still, I think, would be to rush Black off the West boundary about level with the 2nd hoop. It does not matter if a ball goes off the court on a rush, but neither of the balls must go off on a croquet-stroke or your turn will end. You will find it convenient to measure the yard with your mallet as it is important to be accurate. Now you can take croquet from Black and with a half stop-shot send Black to the 3rd hoop and Blue to Yellow. This is really the easiest of the various ways of getting Black to the 3rd, since it does not matter very much where Black went off on the West boundary, or even whether it went off at all, so long as it was somewhere on that side of Yellow. From anywhere in that general part of the court it is easy to get Black over to the 3rd hoop and Blue to Yellow.

You will also see that there has been one main thought in our mind all the time—to get Black to the 3rd hoop. This brings us to one of the most important rules in playing a break and trying to get one established— send the ball to the *next hoop but one*. This is known as the pioneer ball, and if you get this ball accurately placed you need never break down.

Having done this you roquet Yellow at the 2nd hoop, and approach and make the hoop as you did in the two-ball break. Now rush Yellow off the North boundary somewhere behind the 3rd hoop, bring it on to the yard-line of course, and stop-shot it to the 4th hoop so that Blue stops near Black at the 3rd. And so the break continues, after the 3rd hoop sending Black to the 5th, after the 4th sending Yellow to the 6th and so on, always to the next hoop *but one*.

Four-ball Break

Easier than either the two- or three-ball break is the four-ball break, although it is a little confusing to the beginner because, instead of making straight for the next hoop, one makes various detours around the court *en route* for it. The starting position is exactly the same as for the three-ball break, but this time place Red about three yards to the left (West) of the peg.

Approach and run the 1st hoop as before. Then roquet Black gently and send it to the 3rd. Now, instead of being faced with a fairly big split-shot in order to get over to Yellow at the 2nd, you need only play a moderate roll to get Blue to Red. You can be anywhere within a yard or two of Red, although ideally you should stay on the South side of it. Roquet Red gently and take off to Yellow, leaving Red roughly where it is, but perhaps getting it somewhere between the peg and the 6th hoop. Make the 2nd hoop off Yellow, roquet it gently, and another half-roll will send Yellow to the 4th and Blue to Red. Again you roquet Red and take off to Black at the 3rd, leaving Red more or less by the peg and preferably a little to the East of it. And so it continues, as before sending the ball with which you have just made a hoop, to the next hoop but one (the pioneer ball), while going to the pivot ball in the centre and then taking off from the pivot ball to the ball waiting at your next hoop.

Notice that the pivot ball moved around the peg so that it was always on the same side as your hoop. It can in fact move quite a lot if you prefer. You can keep it always between your two hoops. For instance, when making the 1st hoop the pivot ball might be directly between the 1st and 2nd and, when approaching the 2nd, instead of taking off from the pivot ball a gentle split will send it to a spot between the 2nd and 3rd, and so on.

It is also possible to have the pivot ball going round with you—to have two balls at every hoop you make, in fact. This, however, is carrying things a bit far and should only be done if you are playing very badly and want to get your confidence.

End of the Break

If you are able to make an all-round break with your first ball you must not, after making the Rover, peg this ball out, for if you did, it would be out of the game and it is normally quite a serious disadvantage to be left with only one ball against your opponent's two. If you are lucky enough to go all round, you then set up a break for your other ball, hoping that your opponent will miss the long shot which is all you are going to offer him, and if so, repeat the process next turn, going round with your second ball and finally pegging both balls out at the end of the turn.

Of course, the breaks we have been considering were rather easy because we set them up in a perfect position. Although it is very nice to be 'given' a break like this we cannot rely on it happening and we certainly cannot rely on such gifts to help us win our games. We have got to be able to manœuvre the balls into a break, often from the most unpromising positions, so that we can go round, and it is a player's ability to pick up a break from nothing that makes him a good player. One situation where this position nearly always occurs is the beginning of the game, so perhaps it is time to consider the opening.

Back to the beginning

You will remember that there are two baulk-lines on the court, the A baulk on the South boundary and B baulk on the North boundary. It is from these that the balls are played into the game.

The Toss

The players start by tossing, the winner having the choice either of playing first or second, or alternatively of choosing which balls he will play with. (It may be surprising but some players really feel uncomfortable if they are not playing with their favourite colours, and it is a very good thing to avoid getting into this situation.) When the winner of the toss has made his choice, either of start or balls, the loser has the choice of balls or lead accordingly.

The Opening

Nearly all games begin in the same way, for experienced players do not like putting their balls into the middle of the court if they can avoid it. But if you are a beginner who has never seen a game begin, your first reaction will probably be to shoot for the 1st hoop, and if you are playing against a beginner there is no reason why you should not do so.

But consider what would happen if you were playing against an experienced player and you began by shooting at the 1st hoop. To begin with, the odds against running the 1st hoop from the yard-line are definitely against you. The chances are, therefore, that you will either stick against the wire or bounce back a few inches. Your opponent now plays and has a very good chance of hitting your ball and being able to approach the 1st hoop and make it. One up to your opponent, therefore, and it need not have happened.

Most players seem to think it an advantage to go in first, but I do not believe there are any rules about this. It depends very much on how good a shot your opponent is and to a rather lesser extent on how good a shot you are yourself. If neither of you are good shots it probably is better to play first, but otherwise it is doubtful whether it makes any difference at all. For the moment, then, let us assume that you decide to go in first.

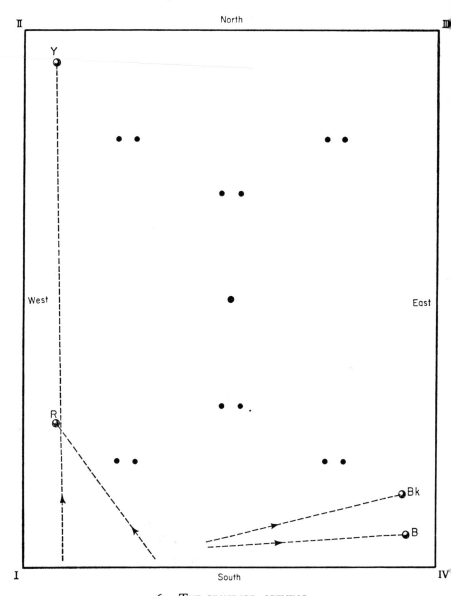

6   THE STANDARD OPENING

Yellow, playing fourth, shoots at Red from the 1st corner, so as to end up in the 2nd corner if he should miss

The standard opening is for you to shoot your ball, let us say Blue, off the East boundary about two yards from the 4th corner. Your opponent now plays his first ball, say Red, about 10 yards up the West boundary from the 1st corner. (It is easier to play this from somewhere in front of the 1st hoop so that the ball crosses the line at a less acute angle, which makes it easier to get it off at the exact spot chosen.) The purpose of this is to tempt you to shoot at this ball by placing it near enough for you to have a chance of hitting but far enough for there to be every chance of missing. For this reason it is known as a tice, for a 10-yard shot is an enticing one.

We will assume for the moment that you do not rise to the bait your opponent has put out for you, and you therefore play your partner ball Black over to Blue, sending it off about a yard from Blue.

Your opponent must now shoot with Yellow at Red, for if he shoots at Blue and Black and misses he will give you immediately a third ball, with which it will be too easy to get a break going. He therefore shoots at Red and, instead of playing as before from in front of the 1st hoop, he must shoot from the 1st corner so that if he misses he will end up as far away from Red as he can get, in the 2nd corner, since again he would be giving you too easy a chance of getting a break going if he were to leave two balls near the 1st hoop.

This business of thinking what will happen if you miss is one of the most important elements in croquet. Whenever you take a shot in an attempt to gain the innings you must think where the balls will be at the end of the stroke if you should miss and therefore what chance that will give to your opponent. Not 'What do I gain if I hit?' but '*What do I give away if I miss?*'

Let us for a moment see why it would be wrong for Yellow to shoot at Red so as to stay near it. If he had done so Yellow would probably come on to the court about a yard past Red. You, playing Blue and Black, want the 1st hoop and you have two balls quite near your hoop. It is a simple matter for you to roquet Black with Blue and take off to Red. You can now roquet Red and a little take-off will get you a perfect rush on Yellow to your hoop. But this, although it should give you your hoop, is not very good play, because you have forgotten to think ahead.

Getting to your hoop is almost the last thing you should think of when you start a turn. Of course it is always in your mind and it governs your whole play, but it will usually be the third ball you roquet which will take you to your hoop. What is important is what we do with the first two balls we roquet. Sometimes it will not be possible to do very much if the balls are in a difficult position, but in this case the balls are relatively easily placed, even though they are all on the boundary.

We know we can make the 1st hoop off one of the opponent's balls, so our first thought is to get one of the other balls to the 2nd hoop. We shall then have established a three-ball break. It may not be possible to get it right to the hoop, but it will help a great deal if we can get it somewhere near or even out towards the middle of the court.

In this case there are two possibilities. If you are not too experienced a player the best course is to take off from Black as described above, and roquet Red. But instead of taking off to get your rush on Yellow to the 1st hoop, a stop-shot will send Red most of the way towards the 2nd hoop. The great thing is to get it in the general direction of that hoop and well in from the boundary—at least four yards, preferably more. Then after making the 1st hoop it is fairly simple to send Yellow to the 3rd and get your rush on Red to the 2nd.

When you have become more proficient you should play this turn rather differently. Instead of taking off from Black in the 4th corner you should play a split-roll, sending Black to the 2nd hoop and Blue over to Red and Yellow. Although this is not an easy shot even for an expert player, it is one that should be played by anyone with a reasonable amount of experience. You have now got a ball to the 2nd straightaway, and by bringing Red in a few yards while you get your rush on Yellow, you have established a four-ball break before making the 1st hoop.

But all this, of course, has been based on the supposition that your opponent has played a shot that he should not have taken. Let us see what we should do if your opponent has taken the shot at the tice from the 1st corner and missed, so that Blue and Black are near the 4th corner, Red is about 10 yards down the West boundary from the 1st corner, and Yellow is in the 2nd corner.

The play that can generally be observed in this fifth turn of the game is one of abysmal lack of initiative. So often one sees Blue, nearest the corner, rush Black a couple of yards up the boundary and then leave a rush to the 1st hoop 'wired' from Red by the 4th hoop. What is gained by this is difficult to see, for Red will remove himself to one of the other boundaries and then, if you do make the 1st hoop, you have little prospect of making any more. It is also quite common for the 'wired' rush to be in fact not quite wired at all; then your opponent will most certainly shoot at you, and it is surprising how often he will hit.

The alternative of going out to pick up a break from this somewhat unpromising position is, although not easy, free from any particular danger.

The Fifth Turn

The correct play for the fifth turn is as follows. Blue should rush Black hard down to the 3rd corner. Admittedly, many things can go wrong with this rush, and this applies to all the shots we shall play in our attempt to pick up this break. But we will consider each possible error as it may arise and see what can be done to retrieve the situation, for none of them need be fatal mistakes.

Our rush to the 3rd corner may go off the boundary after a few yards. In this case our attempt has failed straightaway and we shall have to resort to leaving a wired rush to the 1st hoop. On the other hand, it may go into the court somewhere near the stick and this is not too bad a position, as it is not too difficult a shot to split Black to the 3rd corner and send Blue to Yellow in the 2nd corner. Easiest of all, of course, would be to take off to Yellow, but this would mean leaving Black in the middle of the court and, if anything should go wrong on future strokes, we could not join up with Black without leaving our two balls in the middle of the court. With a little luck our rush should send Black somewhere between the 3rd hoop and the corner; a few yards in from the boundary is ideal. From now on there is no difficult stroke to play. All we have to do is to take off to Yellow. It is senseless to try to get behind Yellow, since we should be most likely to go off. It is quite sufficient to stop a couple of yards short of Yellow, and it will help considerably if, when roqueting Yellow, we can cut it a little to the left, two feet out of the corner. Now all we have to do is to take off to Red. There are two things we should aim to do on this stroke. One is to take off rather thickly so that Yellow comes in two or three yards. The other is to send Blue a yard short of Red and if possible just inside the yard-line area.

It is a very good thing to know your boundary on this stroke. Some boundaries are notoriously untrue, and if you know that it tends to roll out you should play a little inside the yard-line. But apart from this hazard it is not a difficult stroke to play, and has a good chance of giving you a rush of some sort either to the 1st hoop or the 1st corner. At any rate, it is likely to be a reasonable cut rush to somewhere near the 1st hoop, and even if we do not rush it very near the 1st hoop we can safely try an approach to the hoop, as the other balls are safely near the boundaries and if our approach is a poor one we can return to Black in the 3rd corner.

But let us assume that we make the hoop. We may go through, getting a rush to the 2nd corner. We can then rush Red to that corner and a stop-shot will send it towards Black or the 3rd hoop and give us our

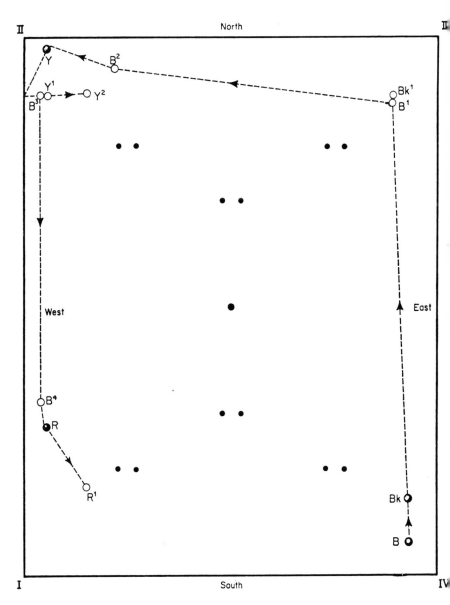

7 *The fifth turn*

rush on Yellow to the 2nd. Better than this would be to have a rush to the 3rd corner after running the 1st hoop, for then we can rush Red to the corner, stop-shot it to the 3rd hoop, getting a rush on Black to Yellow, and then rush Yellow to the 2nd—our break is established straightaway.

But it may be that we ran past Red when making the 1st hoop; in this case we must take off to Black and from there take off to Yellow, sending Black in nearer the 3rd hoop. It is likely in this case that we shall have a hard approach to the 2nd hoop, probably from somewhere near the corner, but again there is no danger, because if the approach does not come off we can join up with Black, leaving our opponent's balls separated and possibly even with a position in which he cannot shoot.

This description has probably seemed rather complicated, but in theory it is simplicity itself, although in practice some degree of skill is needed and perhaps a little luck as well. All that we have done is to rush Black to the 3rd corner, then to go to Yellow in the 2nd and Red by the 1st hoop, working round and up to our hoop and hoping to get the balls a few yards in from the boundary as we leave each one. At any stage, if a shot is not good enough, we can retire to Black, and we should by now have learnt an important lesson to be observed when picking up a break —*do not bring your partner ball into the court until you have established, or nearly established, a three-ball break.* This is likely to be the only piece of defensive play I shall ever advocate. It is not playing 'Aunt Emma' to do this; it is merely prudent. It is being Aunt Emma to leave your partner on the boundary after you have established a break. Croquet is a difficult enough game with four balls and there is no point in making it even more so by allowing yourself only three. Far too many players play every game in a defensive instead of an attacking frame of mind. I have sometimes been accused, and usually with every justification, of being too adventurous in my play. And yet the number of games I have lost directly because of some ambitious attempt of this kind can be counted on the fingers of one hand.

All that we have just considered was on the assumption that the tice was missed on the 4th shot. But another situation commonly arises when our opponent hits the tice, so let us put ourselves in his position.

The Fourth Turn

One of two things normally happens when we hit the tice. We either hit it off the boundary fairly near or we cut it into the court. If we are very lucky we may hit it towards the 2nd hoop. Wherever it goes we have no choice but to take off to our opponents in the 4th corner. If we are taking

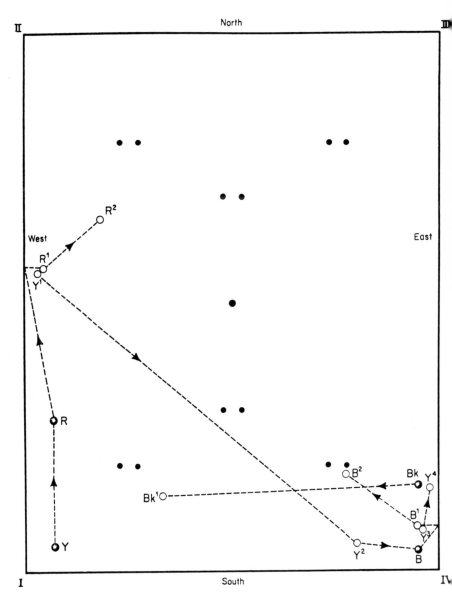

8   *The fourth turn*

off from the yard-line, we have only to play a thick take-off to send the tice ball towards the 2nd hoop. Having done so, we should roquet the ball nearer the corner (in this case, Blue), and stop-shot it into the court a few yards, getting a rush on Black to the 1st hoop. When taking off to two balls in a corner or near the yard-line, always roquet the ball nearer the corner or the yard-line so that you can get it more into the court and come up behind the other ball for your rush. Whilst this is a general rule to follow, do not regard it as one that should never be broken. It would be the height of folly if we were five yards short on our take-off and we did not shoot for the nearer ball.

If our rush on Black to the 1st hoop comes off fairly well, we can approach and make the hoop. If it is not near enough to be worth trying the approach, we can either take off to our partner near the 2nd, leaving Black near the 1st, or split Black to the 3rd and go to Red. Although it is useful to leave an opponent ball near your hoop, in this case it may leave Black a 'free' shot through your balls to the safety of the 2nd corner. In this case it may be better to split Black to the 3rd hoop so that a shot by Black at your balls can be picked up by you afterwards.

But let us suppose that your rush to the 1st hoop went fairly well. As Blue is a few yards out of the 4th corner, you should approach the hoop putting Black to the right, so that when you have gone through you may get a rush back to the 4th corner. If you manage to do so, and to rush Black into the 4th corner after making the hoop, you can then send Black further into the court—probably to the 4th hoop is best—and get a rush on Blue to the 2nd corner. Rush it there, and you can then send it to the 3rd hoop, make the 2nd off Yellow and your break is complete.

It may be that when making the 1st hoop you do not get a rush to the 4th corner, in which case there is no point in going over to Blue. In this case you must play the split-shot to the 3rd hoop, going to your partner at the 2nd. If Red is near the 2nd hoop this should not be very difficult but, if you were not able to get Red in much from the boundary when you took off to the 4th corner at the beginning of your turn, it will be difficult to get behind it now for a rush to your hoop. This is an instance where it would be quite correct play to try for the rush, since if you go off no harm is done. If you do not get the rush, you can choose whether to approach the hoop from the boundary or lie up in the 2nd corner. Which you choose will depend on your ability. If you are fairly confident that you may get position, then you should try the hoop, but if not, it is wiser to avoid giving your opponent a free shot to the boundary, and it is therefore safer to lie up in the 2nd corner. In any case, you have virtually got the break out by now and there is no need for me to go into further detail about it.

So far we have seen two attempts at picking up a break from a position that was not particularly easy. The great joy of croquet is that we so frequently come across situations which are new to us and which have to be thought out afresh each time, so that our experience is for ever widening. Now that you have seen the opening and how a break is played, let us go into some of the refinements that will turn you into something like a croquet player.

The standard grip. Note that the hands are together

The Irish grip. Fingers of both hands are pointing down; hands may be interlocked

The Solomon grip. Knuckles of both hands face forwards

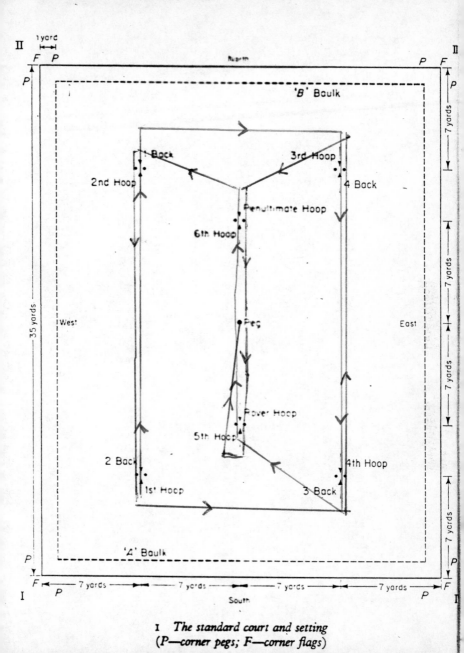

1 *The standard court and setting*
(*P—corner pegs; F—corner flags*)

That 'difficult' stage

Probably the hardest time for the beginner is when he has grasped the fundamentals of the game and knows what he is trying to do, but finds that it is very much more difficult than he had at first realised. The beginner usually sees the light quite suddenly, for in the early stages he understands the principles but does not understand about half the shots that are played between making each hoop. Suddenly, however, he realises the full extent of what can be done and why it is done, and then is frustrated because he has not the skill to do it himself, or the complete knowledge of the easiest way to set about it.

One of the greatest mistakes that beginners make is when they set out to separate their opponents and lie up for next time. They separate the opponents all right, but they never get a good leave for themselves because they are always playing their last shot from the other side of the lawn, and thus rarely get a rush to anywhere. Consequently, next turn they cannot make their hoop and are again faced with the prospect of taking off to the other end of the court to separate the opponents, who have joined up again; the same process continues for several turns. This position is not really difficult—all they have to do is to roquet one opponent, get a rush on the other to wherever they wish to leave it, rush it there and take off back to mother. If they play a good take-off, they should be within two or three yards and can leave themselves an accurate rush to their hoop.

It is the beginner's failure to leave himself a rush that makes the game more difficult than it need be. Even an expert will find it more difficult to get a break going if he does not have a rush to somewhere useful and, whereas the expert may be able to get going if his rush is a very long one (by which I mean that his two balls are a long way apart), the beginner needs a dolly rush and one that is pretty accurately lined up on the spot he wants.

It is also important to decide where is the best place to have your rush to. Sometimes it is better to have the rush to your hoop, sometimes to another ball. Which, will depend upon the placing of the balls. If you are for the 2nd hoop, for instance, and you are laid up in the 2nd corner, it would clearly be wise to make your hoop first and then see how things turn out. If, however, you are laid up in the 4th corner and your opponents are anywhere except, perhaps, the 1st corner, it would probably be wiser to play your rush to one of the opponent's balls. But a lot depends on how much skill you have acquired, for in picking up a break two shots are vital, the rush and the croquet-stroke; the latter may be a split-shot or a roll in which you have to get the croqueted ball to your next hoop but one *and* get an *accurate* rush on another ball to your hoop.

The way to make your break easier is to make sure you have four balls to play with. Often when you manage to get the innings you find that one of the balls is stuck in a corner and you have the problem of how to get it out. You may be able to play a three-ball break quite confidently, but apart from making it easier with four balls you will have to get it out at some stage if you are going to get a satisfactory leave. Let us consider each corner in turn.

Ball in 1st corner. The first opportunity to bring this in is after making the 4th hoop. Rush the ball with which you have made the 4th into the middle, take off to the 1st corner and from there split the ball in the corner to the 6th, going to the 5th yourself. With this shot it is vital that the 5th-hoop ball is *very* well placed. It is not easy to pick up the ball in the 1st corner in this way and, if your pioneer is not well placed, it is far better to carry on with only three balls and pick it up before making 2-back. In that case it is a simple matter to split it to 3-back before making your hoop.

Ball in 2nd corner. This can of course be pulled into the court quite easily before making the 2nd hoop, but if your break is not well enough organised at that stage, leave it until you get to 1-back, when you can stop-shot it up to 2-back as your pioneer after making the 6th. Failing this, your only opportunity will be after 4-back, when it would normally be a little late were it not for the fact that you may need to get it out in order to get a good leave, or to help with a peg-out.

Ball in 3rd corner. Before making the 3rd hoop is the obvious place, but other alternatives are: before the 6th, before 1-back (though this is rather difficult even for first-class players) and before (or after) 4-back.

Ball in 4th corner. Before the 4th hoop, or after it if the ball at the 5th is well placed, or before 3-back are the best opportunities.

In all these cases the corner ball is treated as the pioneer and sent to the next hoop but one, as you split to your next hoop to make it off the ball that is already waiting there.

It is not advisable to pick up the ball in the 2nd or 4th corners by this. Suppose that your opponent has stuck in the middle of the 2nd hoop on his partner ball, your Blue is at the 3rd and Black by the stick. You ought to move the Blue and, although you have a fairly safe shot at Yellow into the 2nd corner, you have a much freer shot at Black into the 1st corner. But suppose that Black is also for the 2nd hoop. You would dearly love to hit with Black, but the shot with Black at Blue is by no means free. In fact, it is a very dangerous one, for if you miss you hand back to your opponent the perfect break he had before he stuck in the 2nd hoop, and he may go to the peg on it. And yet it would not be wrong to take this shot. In fact, it may well be the right shot to take. It is a calculated risk—a gamble in which you must weigh the certainty of a laid-down break with the uncertainty of whether you will hit or not in a shot which is more than tempting.

Let us take another example. Blue is by the 3rd hoop, Black is on the East boundary level with the 4th, and your opponent has a controlled rush to the 1st hoop half-way between the 1st hoop and the corner. Black is quite safe where it is, and clearly you must play the Blue. You cannot shoot at Red and Yellow, for you can be stopped down to the 2nd hoop and a break can be established. But why should you not shoot at Black? Firstly, you are shooting at an angle and therefore likely to go off about three yards past it. Secondly, it does not give your opponent a break. True, he may get one from it, but he will have to play very well in order to do so. A good player *can* pick up a break from any position, and certainly it is one of the most satisfying things in croquet to pick up a break when you have a rush to nowhere and the other two balls are in opposite corners. In this particular position, if Blue also wants the 1st hoop, I think you should shoot at Black every time.

A croquet court is very large and often one goes on to the court to play one's turn and, standing in the middle of the court, it seems impossible to assess the situation properly. One is surrounded by grass, the corners look a long way away and it seems impossible to decide on a stroke that one knows is right. It is really a case of not seeing the wood for the trees. So often the problem is much clearer when seen from outside the court. One ought in these circumstances to step outside for a moment and review the position, were it not for the fact that to do so would be to waste time. Nothing is more aggravating than to have an opponent who spends the first two minutes of his turn in considering what to do. One should know, certainly in nine cases out of ten, what stroke one is going to make while walking on to the court. It may sometimes be necessary to walk over to one's partner or opponent's balls to verify their exact position, but by working out the situation as the opponent is playing his last shot and adjusting the clips one should usually have decided what to do before going on to play.

There is one common instance where many players seem to be in great doubt about the correct shot to take. This is when, playing fourth, you have missed your tice and finished up in the 2nd corner, and your opponent has left a wired rush to the 1st hoop behind the 4th. Mark you, as I said earlier, this position should never arise, for your opponent should have rushed his ball down to the 3rd corner and attempted to get a break going. But let us be charitable and assume that he did attempt to do so, only just nicked his ball and was forced to lie up.

If you are playing against an opponent of, say, two bisques or more, the problem is perhaps not so vital, for unless you join up at the 1st hoop, he probably will not be able to do very much. But when playing against anyone of lower handicap, the shot you play may offer him a chance of going round. Two different shots are normally played in this situation and both are wrong.

One is to shoot back at the tice from the 2nd corner so as to end up in the 1st corner. This is wrong because so often you do a bad shot (particularly early in the game) and go off alongside the tice. But even if you do reach the corner it is not difficult for a scratch player to rush his ball over to the 1st corner, stop-shot it to the 2nd hoop and get a rush on the tice to your ball in the corner. He has only to get his rush to the hoop and he is away.

The other is to send one's tice ball off the North boundary behind the 2nd hoop or even over to the middle of that boundary. This is wrong because, if your opponent gets his rush to the 1st hoop and makes it with a forward rush after the hoop, he has only to rush it to the 3rd hoop and take off to the ball in the middle of the boundary, getting a rush to the 2nd corner, and in the same way he has established a break. This last shot is the more common of the two, and is taken on the basis that, being so early in the game, your opponent may not make the 1st hoop, and therefore if you are reasonably close together you will have a wonderful chance if he should stick in the hoop. This may be very true, but you are as likely to get just as good a chance by playing safe for a few turns and making things difficult for your opponent, rather than letting him get his tail up so early in the game.

There is only one safe answer to this problem and that is to send the tice ball two yards along the South boundary from the 4th corner. Your opponent will not attempt a seven-yard roquet to pick you up before taking his rush to the 1st hoop. If he makes the hoop, he must get a rush either into the 4th corner or to the 2nd hoop to be able to continue. If he gets the rush into the 4th corner, there is no certainty that he will make even one more hoop. If he does not get a rush he will probably lie up in the 1st corner or, if he is wise, the 3rd corner. Although your balls are now in opposite corners, by going two yards out of the 4th corner you will not be wired and you can join up with a fair degree of safety next turn.

'Outplaying' can present a few problems, particularly if you are of an impatient or excitable temperament. If so, then perhaps croquet is not really your game, for the greatest asset you can have as a croquet player is the ability to view the game dispassionately, even though it may be the final of the Open Championships. If you cannot lay claim to such equanimity, it may be that croquet can provide a very valuable disciplinary effect for you. This has been noticeable in one or two players whose otherwise excitable nature is remarkably more composed when they are engaged in an important game.

Advanced play

So far we have been talking in very general terms, which is perhaps not entirely satisfactory, but it has been my intention to give as broad a picture as possible of what croquet is to those who have little or no knowledge of it. From now on I shall go into more detail.

Advanced play is that form of croquet played by players of championship or near-championship class. It differs from 'other' croquet, so far as the laws are concerned, in one aspect only, although tactically it can be considerably more involved.

The laws provide that, in level play between the lowest-handicapped players, a player making either 1-back or 4-back with either of his balls shall concede a lift to his opponent at the end of that turn. They further provide that, if he makes both 1-back and 4-back *before his partner ball has made 1-back*, he shall concede a contact at the end of that turn. The effect of this is that in the first break players very rarely take their ball past 4-back, but end their turn after 3-back and set up the balls for their partner ball, for the penalty of losing the innings is usually regarded as being too costly.

The history, and the reasons why this law was introduced, are quite simple. Prior to its introduction, the first player to get in would go round to the peg and crosswire his opponents at the 1st hoop. He would then lie up in the 3rd corner, leaving only one ball open (for you must leave your opponent one ball to shoot at if you have used his balls) and if the opponent did not hit this shot of about 40 yards, he had lost the game. Finishing a game in two turns did not happen every time, but at any rate it was often enough for it to be regarded as rather one-sided so far as the better players were concerned.

A law was therefore introduced giving the opponent the option of playing either of his balls from either of the baulk-lines. This, of course, had a revolutionary effect upon the game, since it meant not only that the first player to go round did not take his clip beyond 4-back, but also that he had to leave all the balls as far as possible from the baulks. The usual course is to leave your balls in the 4th corner with one opponent between the 2nd hoop and the boundary and the other by the peg. This leave gives the longest shots possible to your opponent, but it gives him

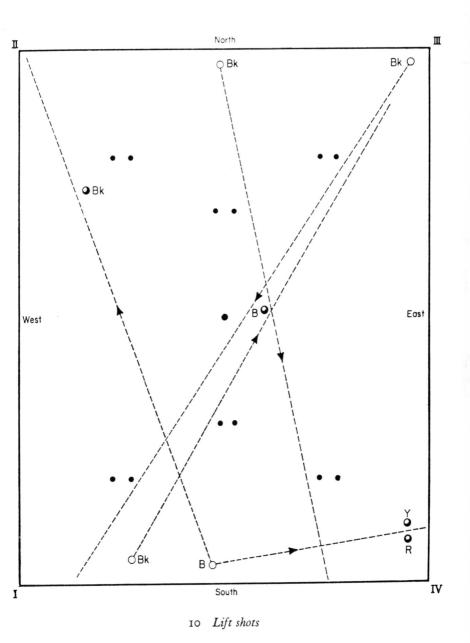

10 *Lift shots*

does not follow that if he is for the 1st hoop you should shoot from the A baulk, for this is where the skill of your opponent must be taken into account. I classify opponents in three ways:

(a) The expert who will do a triple peel and pick up a break from nothing.

(b) The first-class player who will not usually pick up a break from nothing, but will do a triple if you make it easy for him.

(c) The averagely good player who is always likely to break down at any point.

Against (a) I should shoot from the B baulk into the 1st corner or, better still, if the ball at the peg is a yard or two to the East of it, from the middle of the North boundary so as to end up somewhere behind the 4th hoop. To be tucked away there is one of the safest positions against the expert, for it is too far for him to pick you up straightaway, too risky for him to get behind you for a rush to the ball at the peg, and too far from the 1st hoop for him to get a stop-shot approach if all else fails.

Against (b) I should take the shot into the 1st corner and not the shot up behind the 4th hoop, where it would be too easy for him to pick it up after running the 4th hoop. To be in the 1st corner may also tempt him to go for the stop-shot approach—a shot which is one of the greatest myths in croquet, for the number that come off can only be about 10 per cent of those attempted, and every one that does not come off gives a free shot to the opponent.

Against (c) I should take the shot into the 3rd corner, since there is little likelihood of a triple being attempted.

It is becoming increasingly common amongst the experts to peel their partner ball through the 1st hoop when making 2-back, so that at the end of the first break they will be for 4-back and the 2nd. There are two reasons for this: firstly that if the opponents are also for the 1st hoop it is nice to get away from them, and secondly that to start your second break from the 2nd hoop makes it easier to get a triple peel going. Since this is the first time I have properly mentioned the subject of peels, I had better describe how a simple peel such as this is done.

After making 1-back you send the ball off which you made that hoop to 3-back and rush the pivot ball to 2-back. Put it about two feet to the left of the hoop and you roquet your partner (which is for the 1st hoop) a few inches to the side of the hoop. It is best to be as close as possible to the hoop, and perhaps the ideal position is to be exactly beside it from where a little approach shot sends your ball into position and your partner in front of the 1st hoop.

After running the hoop, roquet your partner, if you have not already done so on the hoop-stroke, and line them up so that your partner is aimed directly at the hoop. A little stop-shot sends it through and gives you a rush on the other ball to the peg or to 3-back. After making 3-back it is a simple matter to put one opponent at the 2nd hoop, the other by the peg, and your own two in the 4th corner. The triple peel itself will be dealt with in the next chapter.

The player who is approaching first-class standard often experiences difficulty when he is for one of the lift hoops and the opponent has put one or both balls in baulk. If only one ball is in baulk there should be nothing to fear, for you should safely be able to make your hoop and rush into either the 4th or 2nd corner (the 2nd is usually easier), take off to the ball in baulk and bring it safely into the court. If you prefer, you may find it easier to go first to the ball in the middle and tidy up its position before going to the corner ball. You can send it to a safe place on the croquet-stroke and return to your partner on your last shot, but it is much better if you can do this with a split-shot, so that you get somewhere near your ball and can then leave yourself an accurate rush for your next turn.

If both the opponent balls are in baulk, the problem of making a lift hoop is certainly a very difficult one. In fact, it is so difficult if they are in opposite baulks that it is usually only possible to leave yourself in the jaws of your hoop with your partner in front of the hoop, so that you can peel it through next turn and therefore avoid giving a lift. I am myself inclined to bravado on these occasions, particularly if I am for 4-back and the peg; I attempt to make 4-back with a rush to the penultimate and go out on a two-ball break, leaving the opponents untouched in the corners. It is wonderful when it comes off, but can have dire consequences when it does not.

To attempt this is not only excusable but, if you have the necessary skill, correct play when you are for 4-back and the stick. If you are for 1-back, however, it is very doubtful whether you can or should do anything other than set the balls up for the peel as described above.

There is one other lift shot which can be taken when the balls are in the standard position, and that is the short shot into the corner at the opponents. This is a shot I detest and will always avoid if I can. It has been said that at certain stages of the game it is psychologically right to play this shot, but I am not at all certain that this is so. You get to the stage of playing it (for you are conditioned into it, so to speak, by an inability to hit in) when your opponent is for 4-back and the stick and all set to go out next turn. You feel this instinctively, and at the back of your mind is the thought that if you miss this shot he *will* go out. It is for this reason that I feel to take the short shot into the corner is wrong, for this feeling in the back of your mind is hardly conducive to playing a steady, relaxed shot.

I am myself no advocate of what I am preaching, for I have many times taken this shot myself and will doubtless do so often again. One is, as I have said, conditioned into it by the thought that one will never get in if one does not take the shortest and easiest shot, but I think logically that one should still take the safer shot by shooting at the ball at the peg. The whole question is to a great extent a gamble, for if you play the safe shot and your opponent goes out, you regret not having taken the shorter one. On the other hand, if you take the short shot and he goes out, you wonder whether he might have done so had you played the safer one. This question, and many others which constantly arise in croquet, are best described by these lines from the *Hunting of the Snark*:

> *The method employed I would gladly explain,*
> *While I have it so clear in my head,*
> *If I had but the time and you had but the brain—*
> *But much yet remains to be said.*

More advanced play

The trade-mark of the expert and the ambition of most up-and-coming players is the triple peel. This difficult manœuvre has, perhaps a little, the object of showing one's prowess, but also the very practical advantage of giving one's opponent only one lift shot. The intention is to peel one's partner, which is for 4-back, through its last three hoops while going round with the second ball, and peg them both out. There are three types of triple peel: the standard, the delayed, and the straight triple.

The Standard Triple

In the standard triple, you peel your partner through 4-back when making the 3rd hoop yourself, through penultimate when making the 6th, and through the rover when for the rover yourself, or, if possible, going to 2-back or 3-back.

It is of course necessary to start with the balls at their correct hoops. If, for instance, you make the 1st hoop off your partner ball, it is correctly placed to send to the 3rd hoop ready for the 4-back peel. If your partner is the pivot ball in the middle, it will be quite simple to send it to the 3rd hoop, but if you have to make the 2nd hoop off your partner ball, it will not be so easy to get it over to the 3rd hoop unless you get an accurate rush on it as you run the 2nd.

In one way or another, therefore, you must get not only your partner ball to the 3rd hoop, but also your pivot ball as well, for it is normally essential to have an extra ball at the hoop when attempting a peel. The pivot ball can be brought over after sending the pioneer ball to the 4th. If you already have the two balls at the 3rd hoop, roquet the opponent first and send it a foot or so to one side or other of the hoop and about a yard behind it. Approach the hoop on your partner ball, sending it just in front of 4-back and yourself into position for the 3rd. If you know that you will have enough control to approach from very close you need not send the opponent ball quite so far past the hoop, but it is wise to have it a little to one side or you may be hoop-bound when you have done the peel.

Run the hoop gently, roquet your partner and line it up for the peel.

If you are playing the peel straight, that is without any split, I find the easiest way to aim the balls is to line up the edge of each ball so as just to miss the inside edge of the wire, but if you are playing a split you will have to allow a little for the pull of the ball.

All peels should be played with a steady stroke, more of a little roll than a stop-shot, and firm enough to send the ball through the hoop, even though it should catch both wires. If you have done it well, your partner should be about a yard through the hoop and you should have a rush up towards the South boundary.

You now play a standard three-ball break until you have made the 5th hoop. Some people like to rush back to their partner after making the 4th, but I think this is both unnecessary and unwise. It is not necessary if you send the ball after the 4th about two yards past and to the right of the 6th, and in any case, it is not a nice shot taking off from behind the 6th to make the 5th with so much furniture in the way.

Approach the 5th hoop with a stop-shot to the right of the hoop so that you get a forward rush after making the hoop to the 3rd corner. Rush the ball well over to the East boundary beside 4-back, and stop-shot it to 1-back, getting a rush on your partner to the penultimate. After rushing it there, a little split puts it in front of the penultimate and you make the 6th off the opponent, sending it a little to the left of the hoop. Roquet your partner and line up for the peel. If you are very near, you can play the peel firmly enough to get your partner well through the hoop, but if not, I usually aim it full into the left-hand wire so that, as I am playing a split-shot to the right; it will take quite a lot of wire and stay in the jaws of the hoop. It is much better to get the ball in the jaws than only six inches through, for it is then rather difficult to rush it up to the rover after making 1-back.

Rush the opponent to the North boundary and stop-shot it to 2-back. As you approach 1-back, send the ball to the left of the hoop so that you have a rush to the 3rd corner after running it. Rush the ball behind the 6th and stop-shot it to 3-back, getting a rush on your partner, either to rush it through the hoop and so complete the peel or, if it is already through, up towards the rover.

If you are lucky enough to rush it very close in front of the rover, you can try your last peel now, going to 2-back, but it is not wise to try this unless you are very close and the ball at 2-back is well placed, for the 2-back hoop is such a vital one with the lift pending. More usually, you will send it in front of the rover as you take off to 2-back, and after making that hoop, send the 2-back ball to 4-back, going to your partner in front of the rover.

Here, again, you may try your rover peel going to 3-back, but only if the 3-back ball is well placed, no more than three feet in front of the hoop, since if it is further than that you must go past it to get your rush to 3-back and you may send your ball off. If it is possible, it is worth getting the rover peel over at this stage, so that after 3-back you can put that ball to the rover, bring your partner down to the penultimate, and the balls will be perfectly placed for you to go out on a normal break.

If you cannot do the rover peel going to 3-back, you must leave your partner in front of the rover until you get there yourself, and peel it then. After the penultimate, bring all the balls up to the rover, putting the enemy balls one each side of the hoop and about a yard behind, and rush your partner into position for the peel.

Whether you play the peel with an Irish Peel, sending both balls through in one stroke, or in two shots, is a matter of personal preference. I dislike the Irish Peel unless I am very close to the hoop, and far prefer to peel my partner with a little stop-shot and go through myself on the next stroke. You must be very careful not to roquet your partner as you go through or your chances of pegging out will be very slim, and the triple peel does not count unless it is completed in one turn.

After running the hoop, roquet one of the opponents and get your rush on your partner ball to the peg. Even when things look easy, it is wise to send the opponent balls away, one to the 4th hoop and the other towards the 2nd, so that you do not leave the earth to your opponent should you fail the peg-out.

If your partner is right behind the rover, it is not easy to rush it near enough to the peg to be sure of pegging out, but it is not difficult, if you have both the opponent balls near, to cannon your partner away from behind the hoop with one of them and then get your rush to the peg off the other.

Another difficulty that can arise at the rover peel is that your partner goes through the hoop only about six inches or so, and it is then almost impossible to run the hoop yourself without at the same time roqueting your partner. You can overcome this by previously placing one of the opponents well down to the South boundary, so that if this situation occurs you can jump through the rover, over your partner, and then do not have a return roquet which you might easily miss. I find it is worth putting this ball down towards the boundary as a standard procedure when doing the rover peel, even if I have complete control of the peel. If all goes well and there is no need to jump through, you can still cannon the partner away with the nearer opponent ball and get your rush to the peg off the one near the boundary. All sorts of things can go wrong at this final stage of the triple, and I am always getting myself into the most fearful trouble, but it is huge fun!

The Standard Triple—Variation

I mentioned in the previous chapter that many players prefer to peel their partner through the 1st hoop when making 2-back in their first break. One of the reasons for this is that it makes the triple easier to get going, despite your starting one hoop later than normally. What makes it possible is the fact that, although you are starting your second break from the 2nd hoop, you do not lie up in the 2nd corner, but in the 4th. The essential thing in the leave at the end of the first break is to have your own balls on the East yard-line just outside the 4th corner, and as far apart as possible; this discourages your opponent from shooting at you. Leave one opponent at the 2nd hoop, which forces him to lift that ball since you are now for that hoop, and the other ball about three yards to the East of the peg. I thought of this leave some years ago when it occurred to me that from this position you can send your partner immediately to the 3rd hoop ready for the 4-back peel, while you make the 2nd off one of the opponents. My partner, Pat Cotter, perfected it by ensuring that the ball at the peg is at least three yards to the East of it, even more if you like, since the only safe shot open to the opponent is to lift the ball at the 2nd hoop and shoot at his partner from the 3rd corner. If the ball at the peg is near the peg, he will end up in the 1st corner, and the position is then very difficult, but by making sure that the ball at the peg is well to the East of it, he will probably end up almost in the middle of the South boundary.

Now you begin the triple in this way. Roquet your partner gently, if possible cutting it in a little from the yard-line, and split it to 4-back (peeling it if you are very lucky!), getting a rush on the ball at the peg to the 2nd hoop. Make the 2nd with a rush to the 3rd and, having rushed it there, do the 4-back peel in the usual way, getting a rush on the other ball to the opponent in the middle of the South boundary. Rush it off the South boundary, if possible in front of the 1st hoop. From here a little stop-shot will send it in to the 5th, while you get a rush on the other opponent to the 4th, and your break is fully established. It needs a bit of luck with two shots to pull this off, firstly in getting your rush to the 2nd

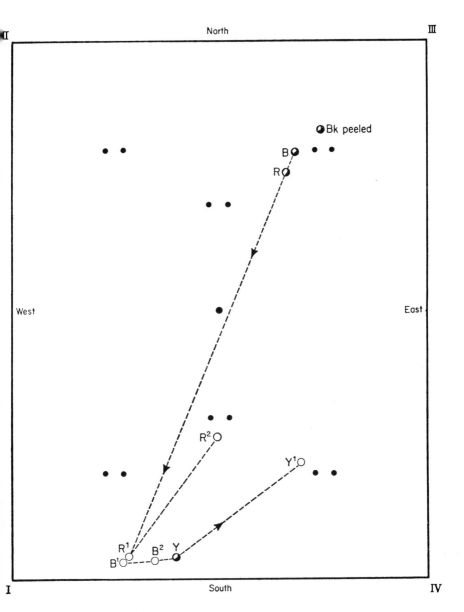

11 VARIATION OF THE STANDARD TRIPLE

Picking up the 4th ball (Yellow) after doing the 4-back peel

hoop so that you have control of the hoop, and secondly in rushing the ball off at the right spot on the South boundary after doing the peel. It has the advantage, though, of getting your partner over to 4-back straightaway, whereas with the normal leave, when you are for the 1st hoop, you would send your partner to the 2nd hoop, and therefore create immediate difficulties in getting it over to the 3rd hoop for the peel.

The Delayed Triple

It may be that in the course of a standard triple one of the peels does not come off. If it is the penultimate it will not matter provided that the ball stays in the jaws of the hoop, but if not, it will mean that we have a delayed triple on our hands. Strictly speaking, delayed triples are divided into two categories—those that start as a standard but go wrong in the making, so to speak, and those that start at a hoop later than the 3rd because it has not been possible to get the balls properly organised in time. The two are really very similar and the possibilities of peeling through both 4-back and penultimate at positions other than the standard ones are very numerous.

If you fail to get the 4-back peel at the 3rd hoop, the first normal opportunity will be to peel it going to the 6th, but to do this you must have the ball at the 6th well past the hoop and a little to the right, so that you can peel through 4-back with a split and get your rush to the 6th hoop. If this fails, you can peel it going to 1-back, which is only very slightly more difficult, although it looks quite fiendish.

You can, of course, peel through a hoop going 'backwards' yourself to a hoop behind you, say through 4-back going to the 4th, by having the 4th-hoop ball at 4-back and getting a rush on it back to the 4th; but this should only be regarded as a rather desperate measure and should not normally be attempted. One place you can adopt this course is when peeling through the penultimate on your way to 2-back, having the 2-back ball beside the penultimate and getting the rush to your hoop as you play the peel. I am more inclined to prefer the split peel going up to 2-back, as one should be able to get within a couple of yards of the 2-back ball, and I think it is more accurate than *getting* a good rush at the penultimate and *doing* a good rush to 2-back. You can do a delayed peel through penultimate going to 2-back, 3-back or even 4-back, if the 4-back ball is a good three to four yards in front of its hoop. But it is leaving it a little late if you have not managed to get it through penultimate by then.

opposite corner and leave your balls three or four yards in from the boundary, with one wired, if possible, and close to a hoop, so that it is difficult to rush anywhere. Then, if he shoots at you, you can use his ball to establish a break and finish the game. But if the prospects of your getting a break out of it are not good, it is better to ignore his ball, go away and wire again, and wait for a better opportunity.

Perhaps your opponent has failed a peg-out and pegged out his backward ball and you have saved the game by hitting the last shot. In this circumstance he should go to the middle of the side boundary, though it is usually worth one shot from wherever you have put him, even if it is a corner. If he does go to a side boundary, being for the peg, you *must* take him away and put him in a corner. If you put him the opposite side of the stick to yourself, he may be discouraged from shooting and go back to the side boundary, which will give you more breathing space provided that you use the opportunity to make progress yourself.

If you are the player who has been pegged out, your tactics will be quite different. Remember that the player who does the pegging out is not entitled to any further lifts, and so you will not have problems of that kind to think about when you run 4-back. As the player of the single ball, you have two possibilities open to you—either to shoot, or to take position. It is possible, though, that neither would be wise, since to do either would give your opponent a three-ball break. In such cases you have no option but to wait on the side boundary, preferably where the possibility of wiring by your opponent is more difficult, level with the 2nd or 4th hoops, and await your opportunity. I once played against a master of the pegged-out game who, although he did not get many wires, always left his balls in such a position that if I shot and missed, he could get a break out of it. Time and time again I had to lay off on the side boundary, hoping that I would get a safe shot next time, while he crept round until in desperation I shot at him. I was lucky enough to hit and win the game, but it might easily have gone the other way.

The Two-ball Game

The position may arise that you can peg out your opponent when his other ball has still a long way to go and your partner ball is nearly round. It may then pay you also to peg out your own ball, leaving only two balls in the game. When to peg out both is not such a great problem. The rules in this case are fairly clear. If you have a five-hoops lead on your opponent, it would be right to peg out both. The two-ball game which then ensues is always amusing for spectators but not usually so for the players. Its result should be, and nearly always is, a foregone conclusion if the player who is ahead sticks to the rules—unless of course, his opponent does some fantastic hitting-in.

If you are in the lead you must studiously avoid your opponent and take position on every occasion. This rule may only be broken if your opponent is for the same hoop (only going, of course, the other way), in which case you can wait a little way off until he has got out of the way. If you are good at getting position for your hoop, you should have no difficulty in emerging the winner. What you must avoid is being side-tracked into shooting at your opponent just because he is in position for his hoop. He is bound to make some, and so long as you make almost as many, you will eventually win the game. Neither be discouraged if your opponent makes two hoops before you have made any. You should if possible, when pegging out, leave your ball near its hoop and your opponent far away from his, but it is not always possible and he may gain an immediate advantage from this. If he makes more than two, you had better look to your laurels.

If you are the backward player the rules are equally clear. You must shoot on every occasion. It does not matter if, by doing so, you end up in the furthest corner from your hoop or from where your opponent is likely to be next turn. If you hit you must remove the opponent as far as possible from his hoop (and from you), but you must be certain to get position for your own hoop. If you are lucky, you may be able to get a two-ball break going, in which case you are in a strong position. It is quite useless, however, just to take position for your hoop without shooting, for if you do so you will never catch up. Your only hope is to hit.

Here, again, there is one situation where this rule can be broken, and that is when your opponent is for the rover and you have run 4-back. If you now take position for the penultimate you are in a threatening position, since your opponent, if he runs the rover, cannot roll up to the peg. He must go eight or ten yards off to the side, while you run the penultimate and take position for the rover. Again, your opponent may not be able to roll up to the peg, as you could risk a shot at him if he is not too far away. All he can do is try to get between the peg and the 6th hoop and hope that when you have run the rover you are wired from him and the peg.

Most two-ball games are a foregone conclusion if they started with the minimum number of hoops lead. But amazing things can happen and one of the most fantastic games I ever played was when my opponent pegged out my ball and his own, leaving his partner for the peg and my other ball for the 6th hoop. I took position; he rolled up to the peg. I ran the hoop almost to the boundary, then hit his ball and took position for 1-back. He rolled up to the peg. I ran the hoop and hit him, and so it continued. I made my hoop and then hit him at the peg on every occasion except one, after 3-back, when I missed. He, however, missed the peg from two yards and I suddenly knew I was going to win, and so I did. I am quite sure I should never win again in such a position—it was just one of those unique occasions. My opponent was a well-known minus player and it was pouring with rain. He had perhaps better be nameless, though I know he did not grudge me the game.

Handicaps

The system of handicapping in croquet is unlike most other games, in that, although each player has a fixed handicap which is reduced from time to time as he improves, he does not play off this handicap, but the difference between his opponent's and his own.

Handicaps range from −3 (the most expert) to 20 (the highest possible), and the system has nothing to do with strokes, as in golf, or shots, as in bowls, or points, as in tennis. The receiver of odds receives bisques, a bisque being an extra turn which may be taken at any stage of the game after an ordinary turn has ended. It may of course turn out to be only one stroke, but if on the bisque stroke you can make a roquet or run a hoop, you may continue your turn in the normal way. A bisque turn must be played with the ball played in the previous turn and in doubles by the player who played in the previous turn.

There is nothing wrong with this system of handicapping, but everything is wrong with its application. If a 10 bisquer is playing a scratch player, the 10 bisquer will receive 10 bisques, and this is fine. But if a 10 is playing an 8, the 10 will receive 2 bisques, or if two 10s are playing each other, neither will receive anything. This means that two long-bisquers playing against each other, particularly if they are of the same handicap, play on level terms, and therefore on the same basis that minus players play each other in championship events. This makes nonsense of the whole system of handicapping, for a handicap is given to a player to enable him to play as well as a scratch player. The idea is that with his bisques, a long-bisquer can go round, taking bisques when he breaks down, and play on equal terms with a scratch player. For example, the theory is that a 10 bisquer will need 5 bisques to get his first ball round and 5 more for his second, whereas the scratch player should make two all-round breaks without any bisques.

There is only one logical way to put this system of handicapping into proper effect, and that is, instead of playing on the difference between the handicaps, each player should have his full complement of bisques. That is to say that when an 8 plays a 10, the 8 should have 8 bisques and the 10 should have 10. In this way, each would have the ability to get on

should be the backward one, for this allows more room for your back-swing before your hand hits your leg.

The real advantage of having your feet disposed in this way is that your body need no longer be rigid but can be free to follow, in a small degree, the movement of the mallet. You are now able to rock backwards and forwards on your feet and this means that your whole stroke will become more relaxed, more supple and, what is of great importance, less tiring. Whether you play centre stance or side stance, or whichever of the various grips you adopt, your feet should always be placed in this way.

Whether you choose centre stance or side stance will depend not only on how comfortable you feel in either of these stances, but also on your success. I feel quite comfortable if I play side stance, but am quite unable to hit anything further than one yard away. Unless, therefore, you feel at home immediately with the stance you first adopt, it is worth experimenting with both to make sure.

It seems to be considered *de rigeur* for women to play side stance and yet there is no reason why this should be so. Certainly, in earlier days it was necessary on account of conventions of dress. But nowadays we are all rather more enlightened, and divided skirts make it quite possible for women to play centre stance. In fact, it is not impossible for slacks to be seen on the court, and why not? Women golfers wear trousers and, although the contenders for the Ladies Championships at Wimbledon are rather younger than the majority of croquet players, they have at least set the seal on a more realistic approach to sporting fashions. If a woman *feels* comfortable playing centre stance, then she should certainly play that way. Whatever your sex, if you are in doubt as to which style suits you best, I would unhesitatingly advise you to adopt the centre stance.

Side Stance

The above remarks about the placing of the body and the feet apply equally to centre and to side stance. But there are certain special features unique to side-stance players which should be pointed out. It is, for instance, quite possible to play with either foot forward. If you are right-handed, and therefore swinging your mallet on your right-hand side, you will probably find it more natural to have your left foot in advance of your right. This gives you very good balance and allows your body to give slightly with the stroke, but it has the serious disadvantage that it is impossible to get the shoulders facing squarely to the direction you are playing.

It is equally possible, and may be just as comfortable, to play with the right foot forward, which has the advantage that the shoulders will face squarely in front of you, but the drawback that the body is rigid on one foot and cannot give at all during the stroke. These are both serious disadvantages in the side stance, and reasons why, if at all possible, this style is to be avoided.

Grip

There are two main grips used by croquet players, the Irish grip, and what may for want of a better name be termed the standard grip. In the Irish grip, the fingers of both hands are pointing downwards, the lower hand sometimes enclosing the fingers of the upper hand, much in the same way as a golfer holds a golf club. In the standard grip, the upper hand is turned so that the palm is against the side of the shaft, the fingers wrapped horizontally round the shaft and the knuckles to the front. Of the two, I believe the standard grip is the better, though I am not qualified to comment to any great extent on the Irish grip. I have tried it on a number of occasions but find it difficult to get any control at all, and a great strain also on the backswing—in fact, I have never been able to understand how anybody ever managed to do anything when playing with the Irish grip.

Whichever grip you choose, the contact between your hands and the shaft must be properly adjusted. Do not grip it tightly, as though it would run away from you if you gave it the chance, nor hold it so loosely that there is any possibility of the mallet slipping in any way. The correct grip was once aptly described to me as a surgeon's grip, firm but resilient, so that you can 'feel' the balls on the face of the mallet, transmitted through the shaft and into you.

Most people picking up a mallet for the first time tend naturally to adopt the standard grip, but almost without exception hold it with one hand at the top and the other about two feet below. Although it may be natural to hold it in this way at first, it is in fact wrong, for with the hands apart it is impossible to get a pure swing. It is the one thing to be said in favour of the Irish grip that it makes it impossible to hold the mallet other than with the hands together. If the hands are apart in the standard grip they work independently instead of together, and the most important thing about swinging a croquet mallet is that one should not be conscious of having any hands at all, let alone two of them.

The beginner must strive gradually to raise his lower hand, not too quickly or he will find himself quite unable to play any strokes, but an inch or so every few weeks. His aim must be to achieve a grip in which the hands are just touching, and at the same time as high as possible up the shaft—just about level with the waist, or perhaps an inch or two below, though on no account higher.

My own grip is somewhat strangely neither of these; in fact, I am almost alone in adopting it. My upper hand is as in the standard grip and my lower hand is exactly the same and touching the other hand. The knuckles of both hands are therefore pointing forwards with the thumbs behind. I used not to encourage people to play with this grip, but I have since come to the conclusion that it is my grip which has given me any success I may have had, or at least, which has made me a better than average long shot. I believe the reason to be that, each hand being held in the same position, each works in a complementary way to the other. Neither hand has any predominance and the result is a perfect blend between the two.

Swing

There is probably more misconception about what a good swing should be than anything else. Most people think it should be like a pendulum, pivoting either from the top of the shaft or from the shoulders. A little reflection will show that neither can be right, for a pivot from the top of the shaft takes no account of the arms which provide the motive force for the swing, and a pivot from the shoulders would mean that the arms must be as stiff as pokers. It is almost impossible to describe in words how to swing a mallet, but perhaps, with the aid of an illustration (page 88), I can give you some idea of what is involved.

It will be seen that the hands should follow a very elongated figure of 8 on its side. The stroke begins only by pulling the hands back slightly so that the mallet rests on its heel. The hands are then lifted slightly, with the result that the mallet begins to swing back of its own accord. Draw the hands back and the mallet will swing back more strongly. Now comes the crucial point. You must begin pushing forward with your hands *just* before the mallet reaches the furthest point on its backswing. Continue moving forward all the time right through the rest of the stroke. At the moment of impact with the ball, the hands are slightly ahead of the mallet head so that the face of the mallet is pointing downwards very slightly, but the head sweeps through on a plane level with the ground. During the whole of the swing the body will sway slightly backwards, then forwards, and for this, of course, it is essential to have one foot in advance of the other or you will tend to topple over and lose your

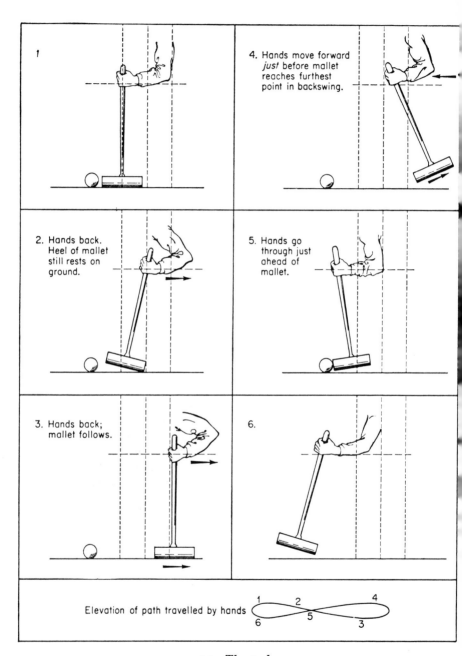

14 *The stroke*

balance. This movement must be *very* slight indeed, just enough to ensure that the body is not rigid. Do not, whatever else you may do, walk forward as you play the stroke—a habit that seems to be more prevalent amongst side-stance players, and apparently they are unconscious of it. The whole stroke is a smooth and steady movement, and the first two stages are so much part of the rest of the stroke that they may not be apparent.

My own grip gives the impression that I use my wrists a lot. This is entirely false and can be proved by holding the mallet only by the tips of the thumb and first fingers of each hand and swinging. If you try this you will find that the swing and the hit itself are unaltered, the only effect of holding the mallet so loosely being that one cannot control the aim, nor can one get a shot with any power behind it.

I am often asked whereabouts on the face of the mallet I hit the ball. I do not think it matters at all, so long as it is nearer the centre of the face than the edge. What is important is that you should not think in those terms, because any analytical approach to the swing itself will mean that you are not relaxed. Relaxation is the key to being a successful croquet player. It is rather like listening to music—there are two ways of doing it. You can listen to every note and establish its position within the framework of the whole piece, or you can detach yourself from it, letting the music put you in an emotional frame of mind outside yourself. A croquet swing should be like that: a movement of the arms that is unconsciously performed and results in a perfect swing. If you have the analytical approach which demands that you constantly say to yourself 'Keep your left elbow up', 'Keep your head down', 'Don't swing back too fast', or such other golden rules, you are hardly likely to be relaxed when playing your stroke. Judging by the idiosyncrasies which some people tell me they have constantly to fight against, it is a wonder they ever get through their take-off drill and are able to start down the runway!

A relaxed swing will also be a consistent one, and you should hit on the same spot on the face every time when playing a single ball. Do not worry if this does not always apply to croquet strokes. I find I can sometimes make edgy shots on roll strokes when I hold my mallet in a number of different ways.

The backswing is as important as the forward swing. It should be steady and unhurried and in the same power relation as the forward swing. That is to say, a hard shot will need a harder and longer backswing, while a soft shot will need a slower and shorter one. But do not worry about whether your swing is straight. It is of course helpful if it is, but some players, and particularly those who play side stance, have quite crooked swings. One of our famous lady players is notorious for her swing which, as it goes back, describes a semicircle. She would not claim, I think, to be more than an average shot and so spent one winter assiduously practising in front of a mirror and succeeded in straightening out her swing. When she got on to the courts next season, she could not hit a ball a yard away!

Croquet Strokes

Holding the hands together high up on the shaft is necessary for single-ball shots, but for all croquet strokes, except the stop-shot, it is necessary to move the lower hand down the shaft. How far will depend upon how far you want the back ball to travel in relation to the front ball. Lowering the hand lessens the resilience of the shaft and makes it possible to follow through the stroke without loss of power at the moment of impact, so that the force which is transferred from your ball to the croqueted ball is not all absorbed by the croqueted ball and is transferred back again to your ball. The further you want your ball to travel the more you must lower your hand, but beware of the pitfall which so many croquet players make. To get the back ball up, some degree of *push* is necessary. This is recognised by the laws, which allow you to push your ball *when it is in contact with another*. Nearly all croquet players, many of whom ought to know better, take this to mean that you may push your ball when playing a croquet stroke. This is not what the law says. What it does say is that you may push your ball in a croquet stroke *while the two balls are in contact*. As soon as the two balls come apart, you may no longer push your ball. Any physicist will tell you that the two balls *must* remain in contact for an appreciable period when playing any form of a roll stroke, but what this period is, is impossible to determine without the aid of the slow-motion camera. And this factor alone indicates that it is a very brief period of time. I do not intend to go further into this, for I am no scientist, but I hope that I have pinpointed the problem for you so that you are aware of the dangers inherent in the roll stroke and are able to cultivate a clean one. In Britain we have always been insistent that roll strokes are played cleanly (so much so that I was always afraid of playing rolls when I first began and would do anything to avoid them), but it is regrettable that this is not observed universally.

Lowering your hand for the roll stroke helps you to get the back ball up, but it is not the complete answer. You must also stand very much

The Solomon swing. (a) Bring the top of the shaft back

(b) The mallet head follows

(c) Hands move forwards and the mallet head follows

Stalking the ball. (a) Line of aim

(b) The stalk

(c) Addressing the ball

further over your ball, so that you are hitting down on it. By hitting roughly midway between the centre and the top of the ball, much more of the force goes into the ground, rebounding into your own ball, and much less is imparted to the front ball.

An interesting experiment can be made by holding the mallet one inch from the head (your upper hand will need to be about half-way down the shaft) and trying to play a stop-shot. It may be a little awkward at first to arrange your stance for this—it is best played side stance, half squatting on your haunches—but if you are able to find a comfortable position you will find that it is impossible to play a stop-shot. If you now play a slight roll you will find that it turns out to be a full roll, and a full roll will become a pass-roll. This method of playing a pass-roll is, I believe, the only fair way of doing so. Whichever method you use, it is necessary to stand well over your ball, even to the extent that your forward foot is quite considerably in front of your own ball. This allows you to follow through the stroke for its whole duration and, because you are hitting downwards, it stops too much initial power going into the front ball.

The Take-off

Beginners often have difficulty about taking-off fine and are afraid of not shaking the croqueted ball. It can be an awkward shot until you realise what it is you are trying to do. You need never be afraid of not shaking the croqueted ball if you are sure you are hitting *into* it, and it is a simple matter to get this right every time. Imagine that you are playing a single-ball shot to the spot you want to take off to, and then arrange the croqueted ball so that it forms just less than a right angle with your line of aim. Of course, in practice you must only arrange your own ball to achieve this, not the croqueted ball, and you have only to aim at the spot to which you wish to go and you will find that the ball will travel along this line. Since the croqueted ball is

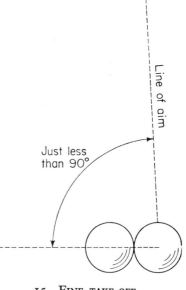

Just less than 90°

Line of aim

15   FINE TAKE-OFF

Ball will travel along direction of aim

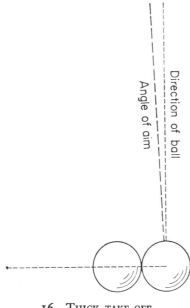

16 THICK TAKE-OFF

This aim will make the croqueted ball move further

just less than a right angle from your line of aim, you must be hitting into it and therefore it must shake. If you. hit more into the croqueted ball it will move further, but your ball will still travel along the same line (which is, of course, no longer your line of aim).

Once you have got the balls adjusted and you know that they are right, forget all about the croqueted ball and pretend you are playing a single-ball shot. All you will have to think of then is the strength, which is enough in itself when you are faced with a long take-off to the other end of the court. There is one final thing to be said about the take-off which is of vital importance. Do not become one of those who can only take off from one side of the ball. Nothing is more limiting to your play than to suffer from this disability. Very often one comes across people who can only take off from one side of the ball—usually the right-hand side. Suppose you are taking off from the 3rd corner to a ball in the 4th. You *must* take off from the left-hand side in this case, otherwise you stand every chance of sending the croqueted ball off the court. It is a hard enough shot to play without giving yourself extra difficulties of this kind to contend with.

Stop-shot

The intention in a stop-shot is to allow as little as possible of the force of the stroke to be retained by the back ball, and to achieve this it is necessary to stop the mallet at the exact moment of impact. For the stop-shot you must stand up and away from your ball, and you may find it most effective to play it in such a way that the heel of the mallet digs into the ground as you hit the ball. Your mallet should not, of course, make any mark on the ground in this or in any other stroke. If you are one of those who make divots in the turf, you are making some sort of fundamental error, but in this shot the heel of the mallet just scrapes the grass and helps to bring it to a halt. This is not in the least complicated to do if you lower your hands (and consequently your mallet) as the mallet head comes up to hit the ball. A light mallet is a great help when doing stop-shots, but it is a disadvantage for the longer rolls or on heavy courts. Unfortunately you cannot have it both ways, for you are not allowed to change your mallet during a turn except in the case of damage.

Shooting and Rushing

These single-ball strokes are the simplest of all the strokes in croquet, and yet they are the downfall of the majority of players. There is no mysterious magic about either of them; they are to all intents and purposes the same stroke. All that I said earlier about the swing applies to shooting and it is virtually all that does apply. The rush stroke is precisely the same except that the strength of the stroke will vary, but this makes no difference to the other elements of the stroke.

One of the commonest causes of failure in rushing is an inability to rush to the other end of the court because the striker's ball jumps up as it hits the roqueted ball. The full power of the stroke is therefore lost and your rush will not travel as far as you intended. There are two probable causes of this, the most likely being that you are standing too close to your own ball so that you are tending to hit down on your ball. It

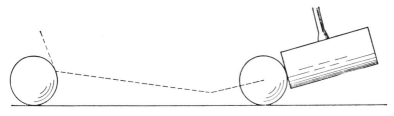

Standing too far forward: the mallet is still coming down

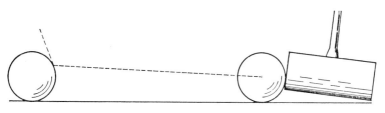

Standing too far back: the mallet has started on the upswing

17 FAULTS IN RUSHING

therefore rises slightly from the ground, hits the roqueted ball just above centre and so bounces up in the air.

Another possible reason is that you are standing too far back from your own ball. This can apply particularly if you are doing a very hard rush, when the tendency will be to stand a little further back if you are afraid that you will reach forward with the extra power of your swing. If in fact you do not reach forward, you will find that your mallet has passed the lowest point of the swing as it hits your ball, and is therefore starting on the upswing, so that your ball is lifted into the air with the same result to your rush. You may have to experiment to find out which of these faults you are committing. I found on one occasion that my ball was jumping up when rushing and I assumed that I was standing too near. I stood further back and could not understand why the fault was not corrected. It was only after standing nearer in desperation that I discovered the other possibility.

There is only one other element in these strokes which must be mentioned and that is the most vital one of aim.

Aiming

I have more definite views on aiming than perhaps any other aspect of croquet. I admit that they may be more successful with my particular grip, but I can see no reason why they should not apply equally to all styles.

Most people aim by standing behind their ball and adjusting their mallet until they think it is pointing in the right direction. This seems to me to be utterly wrong for it does not take into account the most important point of all, namely the position of the body. I aim only with my body and am not in the least concerned with where my mallet is pointing.

I must first clarify this somewhat strange statement by explaining that I always hold my mallet in exactly the same position when shooting, rushing or running hoops. Most mallet handles are octagonal and the ridges formed by the angles of the octagon fit into the hands; in time one becomes accustomed to the position of these on one's palms and fingers. I imagine all experienced croquet players are the same in knowing when the grip is comfortable and natural to them. This being so, when we swing, the mallet will always be in the same position in relation to the body. It therefore does not matter where the mallet is pointing, but where *we* are pointing.

All that you have to do to ensure an accurate aim is to stand well behind the ball—at least three or four yards for a long shot—directly in the line of aim, and walk up to your ball looking all the time at the ball you wish to hit. (There is a considerable psychological element involved in doing this, for it is surprising how often, when trying to hit a ball on the other side of the court, a mere speck on the horizon becomes as big as a football by the time you reach your stance.) When you reach your ball, all you have to do is to put your mallet down, then your head, and swing. You may, if you like, look up once before you play the stroke to satisfy yourself that your aim is correct, but you will be surprised at the success you will achieve without this, and perhaps even more surprised to find that you will be just as accurate if you shut your eyes when playing the stroke. I do not actually advocate doing this—shutting your eyes, I mean—except that in practice it may have the effect of helping you to keep your head down. After all, there is no point in looking up if you cannot see what is happening.

There are many players, I am sure, who in fact follow this practice, stalk their ball carefully in the line of aim, put their mallet down to address the ball, and then look up two or three times at the ball they are aiming at. Possibly they do not believe what they see, as they then correct their aim, but they make the mistake of changing their grip at the same time. If they are facing true to their line of aim, it should make no difference where their mallet is pointing, for it will automatically be corrected when they swing.

Do not worry, therefore, if your mallet is not pointing in the direction in which you are aiming—in any case, you probably will not know yourself whether it is or not unless somebody tells you. If you look at those players who are acknowledged as being the best shots, you will find that quite a number of them aim with the mallet pointing well off the line of aim, and yet they would almost certainly be unaware that they are doing so. The point is that they are consistently off the true line of aim, which only goes to prove that this is corrected in the swing.

Cut-rushes

Finding the spot to hit on the roqueted ball, to cut the rush to one side or the other, was for a long time for me a matter of luck, and I suppose I used to do it by instinct. But there is a fairly simple guide for finding this spot. Imagine a line from the spot you wish to rush to through the ball you are going to rush, and then imagine a ball placed as though for a croquet-stroke against the ball you are going to rush, so that it is touching at the point at which the line emerges from the ball. You now aim for this ball and quite ignore the position of the true ball. This is the method used by snooker players for potting, although it is refuted by

Joe Davis, who says that after exhaustive tests he finds that it is consistently inaccurate, and that this angle is a matter only of intuition. But for all practical purposes I believe it is accurate enough so far as croquet is concerned.

Hoop-running

Of all the vital strokes in croquet I suppose that the hoop-stroke is the most important of all, for no matter how brilliantly you may play in the court, if you make a habit of sticking in your hoops you will not get very far. In essence, it is no different from the other single-ball shots, and all you have to concentrate on are strength and direction. Strength will depend on how near to the hoop you are. If you are within one foot of the hoop and pretty well in front of it, you should be able to run through to any desired position nine times out of ten. If you are much further than this from the hoop, it will depend very much on how you are playing at that moment whether you can play to get through only a foot or so for your rush. If you are really playing well and with confidence, you can play softly at a three- or four-foot hoop and get away with it, but if not, it is not worth tempting providence. Far better to play fairly

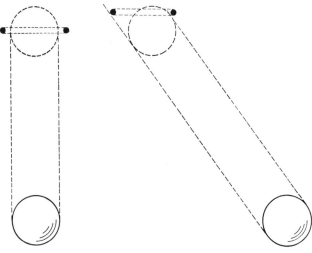

Line of aim—straight. (Pay no attention to centre of ball)

Line of aim—angled. (Pay no attention to left edge of ball. Concentrate on right-hand edge of ball, just missing the wire)

18   HOOP-RUNNING

firmly and be sure of getting through even at the risk of having a long return roquet.

Running hoops from an angle often presents problems to players, many of whom seem to have no clear notion of what they are trying to do. I believe that many players, if they are straight in front of the hoop, aim the centre of the ball at the centre of the hoop, or perhaps at a particular blade of grass in the middle of the hoop. This may be all right when straight in front, but it clearly will not work if you are even a little to the side.

My own method for all hoops, whether straight or angled, is to concentrate on *just* missing the inside edge of the near wire. To do this, I stalk the ball, as in a long shot, walking along the line made from the inside edge of the wire to the edge of the ball. I then play the stroke along this line except that I transfer it to a parallel line through the middle of the ball. There is no adjustment to be made in transferring this line—you will find it comes quite automatically. I cannot myself see any other accurate way of running hoops from an angle, for to pick a spot to aim at with the middle of the ball must at best be a matter of luck. If you can just miss the near wire you will go through. If you hit it, you will not.

When the angle becomes really acute, the only way to get through is to play a jump stroke. Some players have a theory that by looking at the ball through the hoop, they can decide whether the hoop is runable. I have never discovered on what basis they have formed this opinion. Some say that if you can see half the ball between the uprights it is runable, others say you need only see a third. I have a feeling that this fraction, whichever it is, has been arrived at by guess-work. Certainly, although I have never bothered to look to see how much of the ball is visible between the uprights, I have on a number of occasions run hoops which I had written off as being completely impossible, and I am sure that the amount of ball showing from behind the hoop was a lot less than either of these amounts.

The fact of the matter is that running hoops from such acute angles is so much a matter of luck that it is not possible to find any rule to use as a guide. The margin of error is so slight that only if the stroke is right —dead right—will it go through.

The purpose of jumping when running very difficult hoops is to make the ball climb slightly up the wire. This climb upwards gives the ball time to creep *round* the wire and so through the hoop. In extreme cases the ball will run right up to the crown of the hoop, and then drop down, when the spin will carry it through.

I have already commented on page 19 about deliberately imparting spin to hoop-strokes. This should not be done under any circumstances. A properly played hoop-stroke that is firmly and sensibly hit will have all the spin it needs by the time the ball reaches the hoop, since a ball begins to roll within an inch or two of leaving the mallet and this is all the spin that is required. But obviously if you slam at a hoop the ball will skid along the ground for some distance before it begins to roll, and in this case it will go through only if it has been very accurately aimed.

Jumping

It is very easy to make a ball jump and I suspect that most players have done so at one time or another, if only unintentionally. You must stand well forward so that your feet are at least level with the ball and possibly even slightly in advance of it, so that your mallet is pointing down towards the ground. The secret lies in lifting your mallet at the moment of impact so that the ball, instead of being squeezed out between the mallet and the ground, has a chance to spring out of the ground and so up into the air. There is perhaps a knack to this stroke, but it is not in the least difficult to acquire. All that is needed is the courage to hit fairly hard and down, but without letting your mallet hit the ground. You should never make a divot when playing a jump stroke.

It is equally possible, provided the ground is not too soft, to jump over a hoop. The occasions when this stroke may be required are unlikely to be more than once or twice in a season, but I have sometimes found it worth playing when my opponent has cross-wired me. The chances of your hitting a ball over a hoop are as good as they are in a 35-yard shot, and you can frequently end up in a safe corner if you miss. There are, of course, certain requisites to this shot. The balls must be the right distance from the hoop. Your own ball must be between $4\frac{1}{2}$ and seven feet from the hoop and the object ball must be from four to six feet or, better still, more than eight feet from the hoop, otherwise you may be so unfortunate as to get over the hoop with a straight shot, and then be unlucky enough to bounce over the ball the other side. To make the ball rise enough to clear the hoop, hold the mallet high up so as to allow the full springiness of the shaft to help lift the ball.

Peeling

The same principles of aiming apply to peeling. In fact, were it not for the fact of pull which has to be taken into account on most peels, a straight peel from anything under a yard distance should present no problem. If I am playing a straight peel, which I try to do if peeling through the 1st hoop at 2-back, I check my aim by seeing that the two edges of the balls are lined up so as just to miss the inside edge of the wire. Even from distances of up to about four yards, it should be possible to get the ball, if not through, at least into the jaws of the hoop if you are playing a straight peel.

Unfortunately, however, on most peels we are forced to play a split-shot in order to get the rush we want for our next stroke, and on these we have to allow for the pull.

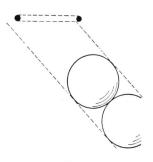

19   PEELING

Line up the edges of the balls to miss the near wire

Pull

This is one of the most difficult subjects on which to give any precise information. It applies, of course, to any split-shot, but on the majority of ordinary splits a slight error in judgment will not be serious enough to make any difference to the break. An obvious example is that of sending the pioneer ball to the 3rd hoop after making the 1st with a three-ball break, so that we play a split-shot to the ball at the 2nd hoop. It is usually accurate enough to aim the ball directly into the jaws of 4-back, so that the pull of the striker's ball will bring the pioneer ball round about two feet and it will in fact end up pretty well in front of the 3rd hoop. It is a fairly safe rule to say that on split-shots of this length, and of this angle of divergence, the pull will be between 18 inches and three feet. The exact amount of pull will depend upon the texture of the grass and, strangely enough, its wetness. Dry grass will produce the minimum pull; with wet grass it will be greater.

For peeling, however, we must be very much more accurate than this. Most peels are played from about three feet from the hoop and, before we can decide how much to aim off for the pull, we must decide what kind of stroke we are going to play. The easiest of all will be a take-off, or thick take-off, since on these shots there is no pull at all. We can therefore aim the balls exactly at the hoop, but there may not be many occasions when this setting will allow the striker's ball to go where we want.

If, as is likely, we have to play a split-shot, the amount of pull will depend on whether the stroke is a roll or a stop-shot. The greatest pull will result from a roll-stroke, whereas a stop-shot will have considerably less pull. On the other hand, a roll played holding the mallet right at the bottom of the shaft will also produce very little pull. None of this may be very much help, for at best the whole subject is a matter of luck. As some sort of a guide, though, if I am peeling from three feet in front with a little roll to the left of about 45 degrees, I will usually aim the right-hand edges of the two balls at the outside edge of the right-hand wire. But whereas this may work, it very well may not, depending on how wet the grass is and how you play the stroke. Why the dampness of the grass should have any effect I do not know or understand, but it is perhaps the one factor in allowing for pull which can be regarded as consistent.

Hammer-shot

The hammer-shot must be used when you have run a hoop in such a way that you cannot afterwards swing your mallet enough to make a roquet. The only way, therefore, to play your next stroke is to have your back to the direction you are hitting, to chop downwards so as just to miss the crown of the hoop, and hit your ball as best you may under these rather trying circumstances. Although it is rather strange to play in the reverse direction, the hammer-shot can in fact be a very accurate stroke, but there are four things to be very careful of when playing it. First, you must not rest your arms on your body. Second, you must not do a double-tap, that is, hit your ball more than once in the stroke (a machine-gun effect is not uncommon when some players attempt this stroke). Third, you must not hit with the bevelled edge of the mallet. And fourth, you must not hit down so acutely that the ball simply slides out between the mallet and the ground. This last is a matter on which referees are often extremely lax, though it is of course initially a responsibility of the player to know what constitutes a fair shot. But without a clear lead from referees, players are often in the dark in such matters. A little thought will show you what is a fair shot and what is not.

Crush-strokes

Crush-strokes, or rather the risks of playing them, arise when your ball is so close to the upright of the hoop that the ball will be in contact with the mallet and the hoop at the same time. If your ball is within about an inch of the wire and is not dead in front, you must have the shot watched by a referee. These shots must be played very delicately, and in the more difficult cases it is quite impossible to get through more than a few inches. But care must also be taken with shots which are dead in front, if you want to go through hard. These shots are very difficult to judge with the naked eye, which is (often regrettably) all that we can rely on from our referees. With straight, hard shots, if the ball touches the wire, the referee must decide whether, in his opinion, the shot was played so hard that the mallet must still have been in contact with the ball when the ball hit the hoop. The eye cannot perceive this nor can the ear distinguish the two separate sounds when a shot of this kind is played hard. This is rather an unsatisfactory state of affairs and it is desirable to have an experienced referee when playing this shot.

The hammer shot. Be very careful not to hit too much down into the ground, since this will squeeze the ball and will be a fault

Practice without tears

Practising can be rather a boring occupation with most sports, since the excitement of the game is lacking. All that can be done is to repeat over and over again the stroke in question and confine one's activities to the rather duller mechanics.

Nevertheless, practice is very necessary if you are to show any real improvement, and croquet is fortunate in that it is a game in which almost as much enjoyment can be obtained from practising by oneself as from playing a game, and this certainly makes a pleasure out of what could otherwise be rather a tedious chore.

The most usual form of practice is to set the balls out in a perfect four-ball break and see how well you can do. But it is vital, if you are going to get the full value out of your practice, to learn from your mistakes and, perhaps even more difficult, to recognise the fact that you have made a mistake at all. It is no practice at all simply to play a break as you would in a game, being content with the poor shots you make and overcoming them as best you may. When you make a poor stroke, put your mallet down to mark the spot you played from, bring back the ball or balls, and before playing it again, think what went wrong. Perhaps the angle of the split was wrong, or one or other of the balls went too far, or you pulled a straight rush to the side. Play the stroke again, concentrating on correcting whatever was wrong before, and play it again and again until you get it right two or three times running. Then carry on with your break until you play another shot you know you could play better, and do the same again. In this way your practice will be constructive.

If you are very much a beginner, it will probably be the case that almost all your shots are bad ones. If so, although it is desirable to practise some of them until you get them right, you will not get very far with your break and you will find it better to play your break normally and, if you break down, to take a bisque. In the early stages of your croquet initiation, the main thing that is needed is as much play as possible, so that you can get the feel of the mallet and learn to expect what will happen when you hit the ball in different ways. Count the bisques you use and do not worry if the total at the end gives you a fright. It does not matter if you take 20 or 30 bisques to get your ball round to the peg. Within a few days you will be taking fewer bisques, and each time you strike a new 'low' will give you a real sense of achievement.

Very good practice for the beginner, and fun also for the experienced player to try once in a while, is to take one ball only on to the court, start from the baulk-line in front of the 1st hoop and take position; run the hoop and then try for position for the 2nd hoop and so right round the full course. Count the strokes you take to go right round. I used to do this as a boy, before I knew anything about the real game of croquet, and occasionally do it nowadays. Although the number of strokes you take in croquet does not matter at all, it is a good indication of the amount of control you have. If you take less than 30 strokes to go round and peg out, you are doing very well indeed.

A similar kind of practice which is fun at the same time is to put your ball on the 1st corner spot with another ball 18 inches in front so that you have a rush to the peg. Rush it up a foot or two and then rush it again, and again, never taking croquet but continually rushing it up towards the peg from wherever your ball comes to rest. If you rush it too far you will have too long a rush and will lose control and may even miss it. Again, count your strokes. Fifteen or under is very good to complete the peg-out (by a rush of course), and I believe 10 or 11 is about the best that can normally be done apart from the fluke of doing it in one!

Games of this kind often feature in croquet gymkhanas, and one of the most useful of these is to put four balls round the peg, north, south, east and west, and about four yards from it. With a fifth ball give your-self a rush to the peg on one of the balls, rush it near the peg and peg it out on a split-shot, going over behind another ball so that you can roquet it and do the same. If you like, you can make it a little more difficult by not giving yourself a rush to start with.

Practice at shooting can be of great value if you can at the same time concentrate on not pressing, so that your shooting becomes relaxed and comfortable. I usually take the four balls to the middle of the side boundary and shoot at the peg, and then back again from the other side, having 20 or 24 shots in all. It is vital to stalk each ball as you take up your stance, to treat each shot as a fresh one, just as it would be in a game. What is surprising in this practice is that over such a large number of shots, your average number of hits will nearly always be the same. I have sometimes hit as many as eight out of the first 12 shots, but I nearly always end up with a total of about 12 out of 24. What is impor-tant in shooting practice of this kind is the number of near misses you have. The peg is very much thinner than the ball, and a near miss would probably be a hit if you were shooting at a ball. The great thing is to avoid those bad shots missing by a foot or more which everyone makes from time to time.

One of the most vital strokes in the game is your approach to your hoop. It *should* not be difficult, because you should have got your pioneer ball very accurately placed in front of the hoop to start with, but we are all human, and the difficulty arises because we have to approach the hoop from so many different positions. It is well worth practising approaches on a clock-golf principle, from positions all round the hoop. From behind, where you will have to take off (practise doing these also with thick take-offs; you may want the rush to the other side when you have made the hoop); from the sides and from the front. Try it from different distances and take care, when playing from two or three yards to the side of the hoop, not to make the mistake of sending the croqueted ball too near the hoop. Beginners, particularly, often aim the ball about two feet behind the hoop with the result that it goes about six or eight feet past to the other side. Aim it at least two yards, if not three, behind the hoop. The wider the split you will be playing, the easier it will be to get the back ball up without sending the croqueted ball too far, and you will be more likely to get a forward rush after running the hoop. Whatever you do, do not be a coward and play a take-off when you know you ought to play a split. If you are approaching the 1st hoop from two or three yards to the side, you *must* play a split or you will have nothing after running the hoop.

If you have reached a reasonable standard of skill, one of the finest forms of practice is to play a two-ball break. This is particularly useful if your time is limited, for in the space of 20 minutes you will play almost every stroke there is in the book. If I have not much time, I always play just a two-ball break, setting up the balls with a dolly rush to the 1st hoop from about three yards in front of it. I must admit that if I do not get a reasonably good forward rush after the 1st hoop, I start again. When I get through the 1st hoop reasonably well I carry on regardless, with the result that in no time at all I am approaching hoops from all sorts of angles and distances. If you can manage to get to the 4th hoop with any sort of control, you should be able to get to 2-back, for the run down the middle and round to 1-back ought to be within the capabilities, more often than not, of anyone with a handicap of about 4 or less. If you get to 2-back, then you have every chance of going right round, but I hope I have not given the impression that a two-ball break is easy. I do not think I manage to complete a two-ball break more than a couple of times a season, and I practise it quite often, since it is the most complete test of skill and control of any of the many difficult things that croquet has to offer. There is, of course, a lot of luck attached to a two-ball break. However good your shot, it is still luck if your approach to the 4th hoop from a spot level with the 3rd ends up really right in front of the 4th. But certainly you will have plenty of opportunity for practising long rolls and approaches of this kind, and plenty of cut-rushes and long hoops into the bargain.

There is one stroke which has not been mentioned until now and that is the corner cannon, and you should certainly not attempt to play one until you have done a little practice on them. I say one stroke but in reality there are several, depending on which corner you are in and which hoop you are for, and they all have to be learnt. Corner cannons look rather difficult, but in fact they are not at all and are well worth practising. The position can arise when you roquet a ball into a corner and there is already a ball in that corner. You have to take croquet from the roqueted ball, let us say Black, while Red, which was originally in the corner, is in contact with it.

There are two ways in which you can do this. You can play the simple corner cannon, in which all you can do is to get a rush out into the court. Suppose you are for the 1st hoop and you have rushed Black into the 1st corner, which was occupied by Red. You arrange the balls so that your ball, Blue, is in contact with Black, and Red is also in contact with Black (but it must not also touch Blue); Blue and Red are pointing directly at the 1st hoop and Black is slightly to one side of that line. The three balls are therefore in a very wide V shape. Now play a gentle tap, aiming half-way between Black and Red, Black will slide out to the side and you will have a rush on Red to your hoop. Before you take your rush, however, you must bring Black on to the yard-line.

This is all very well, of course, but there is a very simple cannon which will not only get you your 1st hoop but a ball at the 2nd as well. Arrange the balls like this: place Blue in contact with Black so that they are pointing straight at the 2nd hoop. Now place Red in contact with Black so that it is $1\frac{1}{4}$ inches away from Blue on the right-hand side. In a match you are not allowed to use any mechanical aids to get this distance and must judge it by eye, but a little practice will get it firmly in your mind. Now, aiming midway between the 6th hoop and the peg, play a slight roll, only a little more of a roll than a stop-shot, hard enough to send Black to the 2nd hoop. You will find that Red goes just in front

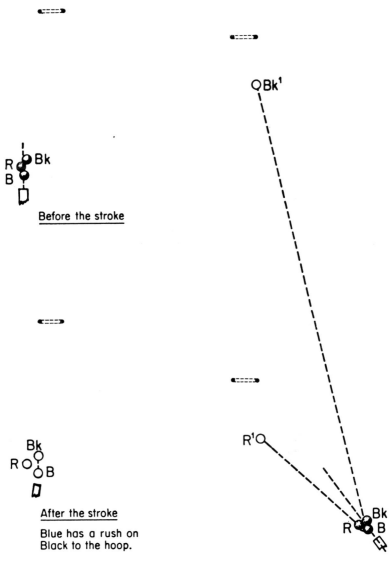

Before the stroke

After the stroke

Blue has a rush on
Black to the hoop.

20   (left) *Simple corner cannon;* (right) *True corner cannon*

of the 1st hoop. What has happened is that you have sent Black to the 2nd on the croquet-stroke, and immediately your Blue left its contact with Black it roqueted Red and rushed it to the 1st hoop. You have made a croquet-stroke and a roquet in the same stroke—in fact, almost instantaneously. This particular cannon is probably the easiest of all and you should be able to get both balls dead right every time.

There are a number of variations to this cannon, according to which hoop you are for and from which corner you are playing. Here are the others. In all cases you are playing Blue, taking croquet from Black and roqueting Red.

1st hoop from 2nd corner. Aim Black at the 6th hoop. Place Red ½ inch from Blue on the right-hand side. Aim at a spot four yards along the West boundary from the 2nd corner spot and hit fairly hard. Black will go about four feet behind the 2nd hoop (which is the nearest you can get it) and Red will go to the 1st hoop.

1st hoop from 3rd corner. Not possible, unless you want to break your mallet.

1st hoop from 4th corner. Aim Black two feet to the right of the 2nd hoop. Place Red 1¼ inches from Blue to the left of Black. Aim two yards up the West boundary from the 1st corner spot and hit just about as hard as you can. If you find that Red does not get up to the 1st hoop, play the stroke with more of a roll, standing a little over your ball, but still hit just as hard. Even on a heavy lawn you should be able to get Red to the 1st hoop, though you may not be able to get Black all the way to the 2nd. At any rate, it is useful to get Black out into the court.

These cannons will give you all the combinations you will need. You will find they can be adapted to a number of different positions. For instance, the 2nd hoop from the 2nd corner is virtually the same cannon as the 1st hoop from the 1st corner. The only difference is that you must play with slightly more of a roll stroke so that Black does not travel quite so far. Other hoops from the various corners can be worked out from one of the standard cannons above.

The laws of croquet

It is certainly necessary to know something of the laws of croquet if you are going to play in any tournaments, and it is advisable to do so even if you intend to play only in your own garden. As in most games, the laws are necessarily rather complicated and you should not be put off if you find them rather beyond comprehension at first. It is certainly not possible to learn croquet from a study of the laws, but it is necessary to have a certain amount of knowledge of them. We will just go quickly through them, and I shall point out the most important ones to you and explain their intentions.

Law 11. If a ball is on the non-playing side of a hoop and so close to it that, when you run the hoop, you roquet the ball before you have completed the running of the hoop, the hoop is scored and the roquet is made. This 'fiction' applies because measurements would otherwise have to be made before every stroke of this kind, in order to see whether your ball would have cleared the hoop before roqueting the ball. *Law 4a* is full of a number of basic factors which are important in croquet and should be studied, but it should present no problems.

Law 12. The replacement of balls on the yard-line is not difficult, but it is very important that it should be done accurately and correctly. Any ball off the court or in the yard line area (except your own ball after a croquet-stroke or running a hoop) must be replaced on the yard-line before playing your next stroke. If another ball is already on the yard-line so that you cannot place the ball correctly, it must be placed touching that ball on either side.

Law 13. If one of your balls cannot hit any other ball because hoops or the peg are in the way, *and it has been put there by your opponent*, you may lift that ball and play it from either baulk. It does not matter if your other ball has a perfectly easy shot; you may still lift the ball that is wired, although you must of course get a referee's decision on the matter unless your opponent concedes the lift. Note that you must be able to hit any part of a ball to have an open shot. You may also claim a lift if you cannot hit your ball with any part of the face of the mallet because a hoop is in the way, or if a hoop interferes with your backswing— provided you have been put in that position by your opponent—but *not* if a hoop interferes only with your stance.

Law 14. Note that a ball does not have to go through the whole hoop in order to have run it. If you cannot touch your ball with a straight edge raised on the playing side of the hoop (your mallet, for instance, although you must not do this yourself in a match), then it is through (see fig. on page 20).

Laws 29 and 30. These appear to be rather complicated but in a nutshell this is what they mean. If any ball is not properly placed the stroke is valid, unless your opponent forestalls you (Law 29). The exceptions are:

Taking croquet from the wrong ball. This is not a fault. When you roquet a ball, you *must* take croquet from it, so if you take croquet from the wrong ball your opponent may choose whether you replay the stroke correctly, or switch the balls as though you had played it correctly (Law 30a).

21 WIRING

A can hit all of B—therefore B is open to A. B cannot hit all of A—so A is wired from B

For breaches of Laws 29 and 30 there is no penalty. If the error is noticed within the limit of claims (see below), the balls are replaced and the stroke is replayed. If it is not noticed, it is treated as having been validly played.

If you play a wrong ball yourself, that is to say that you strike a wrong ball, opponent or partner, with your mallet, you have made a fault and your turn ceases as soon as the error is noticed. The balls are replaced where they were when the fault was made and your opponent plays (Law 28).

All these laws are subject to certain limits of claim; that is, a limit to the time in which a claim can be made that a fault or an irregularity has been committed. This limit varies according to the individual irregularity and each is clearly explained in the appropriate law. If this limit is exceeded, no claim can be made and the stroke is treated as having been validly played.

Law 32. This lays down the rest of the faults that can be made.

The most important and those most likely to occur are (vii), (viii), (ix) and (xi).

Many people think that the wording of (vii) means that in the croquet-stroke you may push your ball in order to play a roll or pass-roll. But the word croquet-stroke is not mentioned. It means exactly what it says. You may push your ball only when it is in contact with another ball. As soon as you hit your ball in a croquet-stroke, the front ball shoots off and is no longer in contact with your ball. There is of course an undetectable period when the two balls remain in contact, during which the mallet also remains in contact—there must be, or it would not be possible to play a roll-stroke at all. But once the front ball has left the back ball you may not push. In the absence of slow-motion photography this is as accurate as we can get, but it is important to cultivate a clean croquet-stroke and not adopt the 'personally conducted tours' and ghastly shepherding' one sometimes sees. It is also vital to avoid any acceleration of the mallet after it has struck the ball, which is a clear indication of an unclean stroke.

If your position for your hoop is very near to the wire you must have the stroke watched by a referee. Your ball must not be in contact with the hoop and the mallet at the same time (Law 32, xi). Beginners often crush through hoops, which are in fact impossible to run, by just banging their ball against the wire and forcing it through on their follow-through. This is a dreadful fault to make.

Law 32 (xii) is rather similar but occurs when you are not trying to make a hoop. You may be right up against the side of a hoop and wish to play down to the boundary. You must play the stroke in a direction away from the wire.

Law 32 (xv) states that if you do not shake the croqueted ball on a take-off it is a fault. But note that, if you are taking off from a ball which is against the wire of a hoop, the croqueted ball may be 'crushed' against the wire of the hoop, and it is not a fault to 'communicate a crush' in this way, for in order to avoid doing so you would be forced to commit another fault, that of not shaking the croqueted ball.

If you make any of the faults in Law 32 your turn ends and the balls are replaced. If you suspect that you may make a fault in the stroke you are about to play it is your duty to ask a referee to watch the stroke, as many faults (particularly crushes) cannot be claimed afterwards, or at any rate would never be admitted by a referee who had not seen the stroke.

Law 35. If the clips are incorrectly placed and you have therefore played under the impression that your opponent was for a different hoop, you may replay that part of your turn which was affected, since you have been misled into a course of play that you would not otherwise have taken.

Law 38. If you say that you will take a bisque, you may change your mind and not play it. If you say you will *not* take a bisque you may *not* change your mind (*d*). If you make a fault, you may take a bisque to continue your turn. If on a bisque stroke you make a fault, the balls are replaced but you have still taken your bisque.

Law 39. In handicap games you may not peg out your rover ball unless your partner is also a rover or unless one of your opponent's balls has been pegged out.

This is only the briefest explanation of the laws and only covers some of the things which seem to me to give beginners the most trouble. In the main, you will learn all you need to know from players in your club, who will put you right if you do anything seriously wrong. I have not given the fullest explanation of what to do if you do make any of these errors. The complete answer is given in the laws, so if you get into one of these situations look up the appropriate law to find out how to put it right.

Developments in croquet

Since the earlier edition of this book some changes have taken place which need now to be included. These concern a new approach to the game by the experts of today in a number of areas, principally the opening and the leaves at the end of a turn. A new approach to the game has also come from the Croquet Association as a result of the enormous upsurge in interest from the public.

With twice as many clubs and members of the Association, and with help from the Sports Council, it has been possible to give a great deal of practical help with tuition and the organisation of new events, particularly those which will encourage younger people in schools, colleges and universities. This has in part resulted in the development of a new variation of croquet which gives the opportunity of completing a game in an hour—important to new players who can easily become frustrated at attempting to play the full game when they have not yet acquired the necessary technique.

Sponsorship has also played a large part in these developments, for the prospect of having croquet on television demands a game lasting at most one hour, which can be edited down to 45 minutes, or even less. We will look briefly at the various developments.

The Experts

On page 29 I suggested that the first player should play a couple of yards up the East boundary from the 4th corner. In recent years it has become much more common for the first player to go off the East boundary about level with the fourth hoop, possibly even 8 or 9 yards from the 4th corner. The reasoning behind this seems to be that it increases the length of the short shot the second player is now more apt to take.

I still have an inherent dislike of leaving the balls so far from the corner, offering a 'free' shot from B baulk, even though this is a long shot. Clearly, if the second player has left a normal tice, on the fourth turn he is almost certain to shoot at the tice rather than at the opponents. But the short shot (with the fourth ball) can be made less attractive by leaving one's partners near the fourth corner, but at least 4 yards apart.

There are other variations played by the experts, and these can be learned from other books which cater for experienced players. The variation just mentioned is given because it is commonly seen today and the beginner may wonder at the reason.

The end of the first break, and the leave, was described on page 52, but this is now known as the Old Standard leave. The New Standard leave is now very often seen and needs to be explained.

At the end of the first break one opponent ball is left at the second hoop, either on the wire or very close to it, wired from B baulk. The other opponent is left similarly on or near the wire of the fourth hoop wired from A baulk. It does not matter if this ball is up to a foot away from the hoop, for your own balls are left on the East yard line, some ten yards from the fourth corner, and although only about 6 yards from the opponent he cannot swing because of the hoop.

If the ball is left almost on the wire of the fourth hoop, it seems a silly leave, since you cannot rush this ball to the first hoop after your opponent has, hopefully, missed the lift shot into the fourth corner. But of course the object is to send your partner to the middle, getting a rush on the ball at the fourth hoop into the fourth corner, and then to rush that ball to the first hoop to establish the second break.

Sometimes elaborate 'hoop leaves' may be observed, when the opponents are left in the jaws of hoops, or against the wire of a hoop or the peg. When these come off they can be very effective and certainly look very clever. But in my observation frequently one and occasionally both enemy balls roll out of the hoop or bounce off the wire and the result is a disastrous leave offering a short shot to the opponents. Leaves of this kind are definitely not recommended to players who have not yet approached A class play and are beginning to experiment with triple peels. They need expert technique and carefully thought out tactics to achieve the desired result.

As mentioned above, the Croquet Association has spent much time and thought in developing new versions of the game which will appeal to a television audience. It was quickly realised that the size of the court was a problem and the first step was to cut the court in half, giving dimensions of $28 \times 17\frac{1}{2}$ yards. The half court size has now been standardised at 24×16 yards.

The very short distances between hoops offer many advantages for beginners and 'Short Croquet', in which the course consists of six hoops and the peg, has now been officially adopted. For the experts who would be playing in televised events the game is very unsatisfactory, because the distances are so short, and therefore compulsory peels were introduced. The lowest handicapped players were required to make 6 peels of the partner ball (in a full 26-point game) and this meant that they could not afford to have one ball too far ahead of the other.

Although this may seem to inhibit normal break play, it is a valuable and interesting form of the game for the experts and games by them are normally completed well within an hour. However, indoor carpets, which are now becoming available, have given another dimension to the half court game. Indoor courts are not only almost as level as a billiard table, but they are also extremely fast. Because the balls seem to keep running almost forever, great skill is needed to control the break and this means that a normal game can be played without the necessity for 'artificial' refinements such as compulsory peeling. There is no doubt that indoor courts will have a profound influence on croquet, both as a means of getting newcomers interested in the game, and in offering a satisfactory way of putting it on the television screen.

The developments in the game since its origins in the second half of the 19th century have been very little, but the few changes that have been made have been extremely significant. They can be briefly summarised as follows:

1913 Wiring lift introduced (Current Law 13).
1920 Option to play either ball at start of turn. This completely revolutionised the whole concept of the game.
1922 Current setting of 6 hoops and one central peg.
1928 Lift after opponent had made 4 back.
1946 Two lifts and contact introduced (Current Law 36).
1986 Authorisation of Short Croquet (half sized court with only one circuit of court).
1988 Authorisation of professionalism.

It will be seen that it took a long time for these major changes in the game to be introduced, many of them after some years of experiment. The acceptance of professionalism (albeit at extremely modest levels of remuneration) indicates that the Croquet Association is aware of the fact that the sport must continue to develop and meet the challenges of today's conditions. Doubtless other developments will follow in due course.

Conclusion

What of the future? I hope I have been able to give some indication of the complexity of croquet and of the skill and knowledge necessary in its execution. If, before you read this book, your impression was that it was a game comparable with tiddlywinks, I hope that this has been dispelled. All tournament croquet, whatever your handicap, is a serious affair, and in the Championship class it can often be nerve-racking in the extreme. The Croquet Association organises tournaments in the major centres in the country throughout the season, and it is possible to play in a tournament somewhere in every week of the season from mid-May until early October. In New Zealand and Australia similar conditions prevail.

The finest tournament organised by the Croquet Association, surpassing even the Open Championships, is the President's Cup, in which the best eight players of the year are invited to compete, and in which each player twice plays the other seven, regardless of whether they win or lose. The strain and concentration required in playing 14 games in five days is a supreme test of a croquet player's skill and I count it amongst my greatest pleasures that I have been privileged to play in this tournament on a number of occasions. If we add to this the fact that it is in this tournament that the hoops are only $\frac{1}{16}$ inch larger than the balls, it can be regarded as the most supreme test of skill open to the croquet player.

Croquet has altered a good deal during the 100 years or so of its official existence. I believe that it should still undergo some changes in the years to come. So far as the expert is concerned there is little or no cause for complaint. The harder the game is, the better it suits him, since, his skill being greater than other players', he is more likely to emerge the winner. But at a time when croquet is attracting a much wider public—and most welcome among these are the younger generation from the universities and schools—it will be necessary for its even wider acceptance that changes be made to enable it to be more readily and quickly understood by beginners. Its only drawback is the length of time needed to grasp the fundamentals of the game, and also the time needed to acquire the rudimentary skill necessary to all except the most natural and gifted players.

The form that these changes could take are many and varied. They have been discussed on numerous occasions over the years and from time to time some have been adopted. So long as the powers that be do not lose sight of the fact that the ultimate interest of croquet will be served if, for the beginner at any rate, the game is made considerably easier than it is at present, there will be no cause for concern. My own concern is that the pleasures I have received from croquet since the age of 15 should not be denied to those who have not the perseverance necessary to discover the joys and delights of what is undoubtedly the queen of games.

Appendix: The MacRobertson International Shield

The international contests for the MacRobertson Shield have unfortunately been rather spasmodic, at any rate since the war, owing to the great expense of sending teams to the other side of the world, and the fact that croquet is not a sport which attracts large crowds of spectators who can help to finance such tours. Nevertheless they have been keenly awaited and fiercely contested, and of the thirteen Series* of Test Matches so far held, Great Britain has won seven, Australia three, and New Zealand three.

Other countries are now seeking to enter the International field, notably The United States, Japan and South Africa. Ireland, Wales and Scotland have their own associations, and croquet is played strongly in Canada and Bermuda, albeit under rather different Laws.

Test Matches in croquet may seem amusing to people who think in terms of cricket when a Test Match is mentioned. I can only say that they are very serious affairs so far as croquet players are concerned, and if you are one of those who has always regarded croquet as an amusing little pastime, perhaps the thought that we are prepared to send teams to the other side of the world, usually at great expense to those privileged to be selected, will tell you that croquet is not the game that you suspected it to be.

* A series can be three, four or five Test Matches.

Year	Held in	Result
1925	England	England 3 Australia 0
1927	Australia	Australia 1 England 1 1 Match tied (Australia won on games)
1930	Australia	Australia 3 New Zealand 0
1935	Australia	Australia 4 England 3 New Zealand 0 (2 tied) (2 tied)
1937	England	England 5 Australia 0
1950	New Zealand	New Zealand 2 England 1
1956	England	England 5 New Zealand 0
1963	New Zealand	England 6 Australia 2 New Zealand 1
1969	Australia	England 6 New Zealand 3 Australia 0
1974	England	Great Britain 6 New Zealand 2 Australia 1
1978	New Zealand	New Zealand 6 Great Britain 3 Australia 0
1982	Australia	Great Britain 5 New Zealand 4 Australia 0
1986	England	New Zealand 5 Great Britain 3 Australia 1

Results of contests for the MacRobertson Shield

Index

INDEX